HOW TO PROFIT FROM BITCOIN

2022

The Best Bitcoin Guide for Beginners

Table of Contents

INTRODUCTION

WHO IS THIS BOOK FOR?

As a child, I loved to collect coins and occasionally small denomination currency notes from different countries. I grew up in a world where the concept of currency was deeply intertwined with the nation-state and national sovereignty, as did most other people. This act may explain why most of us missed out on profiting from early crypto-boom and did not buy a couple of 100 bitcoins in 2011. Of course, those who did don't need this book. Now, suppose you are someone who got interested in Bitcoins after November 2020. In that case, the bad news is that you certainly missed out on the opportunity to obtain Bitcoins when they were trading at $1000 or even $10,000 (which was before September 2020, incidentally). However, while you are late to the party, you are not alone. To put it simply:

This book is for all of you who have come to the world of Bitcoins and other cryptocurrencies late (especially after November 2020).

2021 is the year when cryptos in general and Bitcoin, in particular, have come of age. While we may never see the rock bottom prices of a few years ago, it is still entirely possible to profit from Bitcoins if one moves smartly and sensibly. The key is to move smartly, sensibly and note that Bitcoin investing is not a get-rich-quick scheme. Even if you were fortunate enough to start investing in Bitcoins before 2020, this book could still help you gain a fresh perspective and new ideas as you move forward on your journey.

Before jumping in, there is some basic housekeeping to bear in mind:

1. This is not a get-rich-quick guide. Get-rich-quick guides usually end in tears. Remember the adage, "if you want to make a million

in the market overnight, start with 2 million".

2. The contents of this guide are not financial advice. Please use your discretion or consult a professional financial advisor before making investment decisions

3. This guide is purely educational and designed with the view of helping people learn how they can get exposure to the crypto-assets space

The crypto space is a rapidly evolving field. As blockchain goes on to gain more mainstream acceptance, the pace of the change will accelerate. So what is valid and applicable today may be antiquated tomorrow (both literally and metaphorically, as a lot can change in 24 hrs). So I apologize for any oversimplifications, errors, and omissions. I am not affiliated with any of the products and services I mention in this book. I am just presenting examples of the different products and services to help you make informed choices. The basic structure of the book is as follows:

Chapter 1: In this chapter, you will get a brief overview of the technical aspects of Bitcoins, including a brief description of the underlying technology, blockchain. Now, you don't have to be a blockchain expert to profit from Bitcoins, so you can skip this chapter if you like. However, I recommend going over the glossary of commonly used crypto terms, as you will encounter them a lot throughout your crypto journey.

Chapter 2: This chapter provides a brief historical context to Bitcoins, including the history of its tumultuous price history and some of the current issues it faces. Bitcoins are rapidly gaining mainstream attention; It is still a very volatile asset. While the bull runs are nothing short of exhilarating, the bear turns feel like a punch in the gut. Having a historical context and a knowledge of the current macro environment Bitcoin is operating in, you are more likely to remain calm during the frenzy Bitcoin price changes invoke.

Chapter 3: In this chapter, we get down to it. You will get a detailed overview of getting your Bitcoins and a detailed description of some common crypto exchanges. Additionally, you will learn about some traditional sources that have now enabled crypto purchases. Finally, you will learn about hardware wallets and how they are vital for preventing your Bitcoins from being stolen by hackers.

Chapter 4-7: Now that you have your Bitcoins, you will learn about some common investment strategies and the tools that can help you implement those (chapter 4). Intelligent people don't work for money; they make money work for them. In chapter 5, you will learn about the tools you earn passive income from your Bitcoins. Diversification is the key to successful investment. This is true for conventional stocks as it is for Bitcoins, and in chapter 6, you will learn how to diversify your crypto holdings (and about the 2021 bitcoin ETFs). In chapter 7, you will learn how to profit from Bitcoins without buying any Bitcoins.

Chapter 8: We will finish off by seeing what is next for Bitcoin, post-2021, and some tips to stay safe on this hair-raising but rewarding Bitcoin journey.

I will be grateful for your feedback, and please drop me a line at minerva.data.lab@gmail.com. Further, the Bitcoin and cryptocurrency space are rapidly evolving. You can always follow me on my Medium page to get updated news and analysis on cryptocurrency-related topics: https://minerva-data-owl.medium.com/

You can download your whistle-stop no-fluff guide to profiting from Bitcoins in 2021 and beyond: https://minerva-ea911.gr8.com/. This will be your primer on what to do and what not to do in order to succeed on your Bitcoin journey.

CHAPTER 1:

A BRIEF OVERVIEW OF CONCEPTUAL FOUNDATIONS

1.1: Birth of a Star: Bitcoins Enter the World

Bitcoin is a peer-to-peer system for making online payments using a digital currency. The idea of a digital currency has been around for some time. Still, the concept of Bitcoin emerged when Satoshi Nakamoto posted a white paper titled Bitcoin: 'A Peer-to-Peer Electronic Cash System' on a cryptography mailing list in 2008. Interestingly no one knows who Satoshi Nakamoto is and whether it's one person or a group of people. However, Bitcoins came into existence in 2009 when a small community of cryptographers started 'mining' Bitcoins. While Bitcoin was not the first digital currency to come about, what contributed to its success was its ability to tackle the problem of *'double spending.'* Since all things digital can be copied over and over again, the challenge was creating a digital payment system that makes sure that nobody spends the same money more than once. Offline it's handled by the fact paper money is physically transferred from buyer to seller. Online it's been handled by central authorities (such as banks)recording and verifying all transactions and then removing the payment from the buyer's account and adding it to the seller's account. What makes Bitcoin unique is that it uses a massive peer-to-peer network to verify every single transaction. When you send a Bitcoin to another person, they don't actually get to use it until 'the network' confirms it is valid. Once verified, though, your payments are non-reversible, your accounts cannot be frozen, and transaction fees are usually lower. The advantages offered by Bitcoin in terms of its security is arguably one of the reasons why even countries are moving to adopt Bitcoin (more of that in chapter 2). All transactions are public, and nothing is hidden from anyone.

Bitcoin is completely decentralized, open-sourced, and transparent. This means that you can see all the transactions that have ever been done on the network, and you can check and review the blockchain data yourself to verify the authenticity of each transaction. Bitcoin runs on highly complex mathematical algorithms to regulate the creation of new bitcoins and ensure no double-spending ever occurs on the network (remember, this is the Achilles' heel of failed virtual currencies before Bitcoin). The Bitcoin code is so secure and advanced that it's virtually impossible to cheat the system, so if you think you can create an unlimited number of bitcoins, you're greatly mistaken (and Bitcoin mining is not the topic of this book). Of course, the idea of digital money, especially digital money, without governmental oversight is difficult to imagine. But this is what has made Bitcoin and cryptocurrencies take off.

One of the main problems of traditional currency is that these aren't limited in number. This means that governments and central banks can print more money when they see fit. When more money is printed and enters the economy, this reduces the purchasing power of our paper money, which means we need to spend more for an item we've only spent a few dollars on before; this is called inflation. Bitcoin, on the other hand, is a different story. The Bitcoin Protocol states that only 21 million Bitcoins can ever be mined and created, which means that bitcoin is, in fact, a scarce resource. This is why Bitcoin is now regarded as a hedge against inflation (more on that in chapter 8). But right now, let us learn more about the technology-blockchains that underpin Bitcoins (and make them so powerful).

1.2 What is a Blockchain?

The blockchain is simply a record of all Bitcoin transactions that have ever taken place. It is similar to a ledger in that a bank might keep recording all their customers' transactions, and it is key to preventing 'double spending.' Instead of a central authority such as a bank maintaining the ledger, with the blockchain, a copy of the ledger file is shared between thousands of participants globally who choose to become involved as 'miners.' New bitcoin transactions are added in the blockchain by a consensus of a majority of the miners who earn Bitcoin for their verification services. Once a transaction is entered into the blockchain, it can never be erased or modified. More importantly, it's virtually impossible to hack or cheat the system because that would require the attacker to attempt to modify the 'block' they want to alter and every other block that follows to the present time. And he'd need to do it all before the next block was added after that. The good news, you don't need to do anything or even know too much about all this to use Bitcoin. This massive community is always working quietly in the background, verifying transactions and creating (a limited number of) new Bitcoins. For those who are more cryptographically minded, figure 1 displays how the Bitcoin blockchains work.

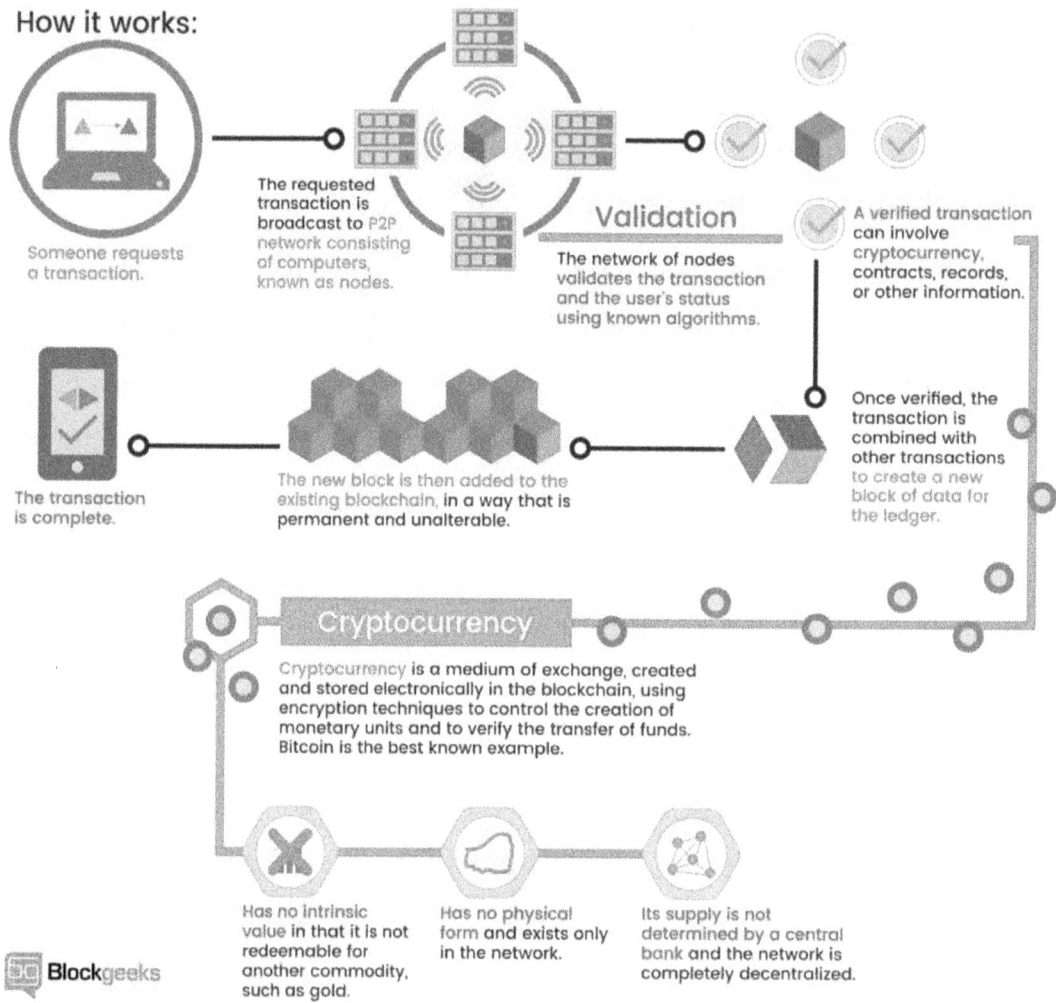

How it works:

Someone requests a transaction.

The requested transaction is broadcast to P2P network consisting of computers, known as nodes.

Validation

The network of nodes validates the transaction and the user's status using known algorithms.

A verified transaction can involve cryptocurrency, contracts, records, or other information.

Once verified, the transaction is combined with other transactions to create a new block of data for the ledger.

The transaction is complete.

The new block is then added to the existing blockchain, in a way that is permanent and unalterable.

Cryptocurrency

Cryptocurrency is a medium of exchange, created and stored electronically in the blockchain, using encryption techniques to control the creation of monetary units and to verify the transfer of funds. Bitcoin is the best known example.

Has no intrinsic value in that it is not redeemable for another commodity, such as gold.

Has no physical form and exists only in the network.

Its supply is not determined by a central bank and the network is completely decentralized.

Blockgeeks

Figure 1: How The Bitcoin Blockchain Works

1.3 Who Controls Bitcoin?

A Bitcoin transaction is simply a transfer of value between two Bitcoin wallets included in the Blockchain. I will discuss the concept of Bitcoin wallets in-depth in chapter 3. So, the only people involved are the two exchanging funds and the miners working anonymously in the background to verify the blockchain transaction. A Wallet is simply a digital storage space that holds your Bitcoin. They are many variations, mostly differing by security measures and convenience, but essentially, they all store your private key, or seed, which is used to sign transactions. This private key provides mathematical proof that the Bitcoin you sent indeed came from you, the wallet owner. That proof is verified each time by the miners who confirm the transaction (using the procedures outlined in figure 1). Various government bodies and banking organisations have attempted to regulate the use of Bitcoin, but the system itself is beyond their reach. The peer-to-peer structure, plus multiple checks and measures built into the system itself, makes it extremely difficult for anyone to manipulate Bitcoin. The underlying software is open-source so that anyone can make modifications and improvements. Any developer with interest can propose changes to the software. The miners then vote on those changes. If they think it's good for Bitcoin, they start using the new version of the software. If the majority start using it, it's the new standard, and the rest of the miners quickly come around.

When you've selected the most suitable wallet for your needs (which you will be after reading chapter 3), you can then start making bitcoin transactions. To send bitcoin to another user, all you have to do is just get their email or bitcoin address, enter the amount you wish to send, write a quick note to tell them what the payment is for (this is optional), and hit the Send button Alternatively, if you've got the QR code to their bitcoin wallet, you can simply scan it and hit Send. The transaction will appear in the other person's account in a short time, usually between 10-45 minutes. The reason for this 'wait' is explained more fully in the next section. And that's it! Bitcoin transactions are quick, safe, cheap, and the perfect alternative to paying with bank-issued credit and debit cards and even paying in cash.

1.4 Some Common Terms you Need to be Aware of

Just before we move on, there are a few terms you'll be seeing a lot of during your Bitcoin journey. So just to be safe, here's a quick checklist:

- Fiat Money: regular paper money as we know it. The central bank of a country issues it (e.g., Bank of England, Reserve Bank of India, Bank of Korea)

- Cryptocurrency: A type of currency that uses cryptography instead of a central bank to provide security and verify transactions. Bitcoin is the first cryptocurrency.

- Bitcoin: The original cryptocurrency. The abbreviation is BTC

- Altcoin: A generic term for all cryptocurrencies

- Blockchain: The encrypted string that records all Bitcoin transactions. Each new transaction is added to the string—the authoritative record of every Bitcoin transaction that has ever occurred.

- Digital coin: A digital asset that is native to its blockchains such as Bitcoin or Ether

- Bits: A sub-unit of one bitcoin. There are 1,000,000 bits in one bitcoin.

- Satoshis: Named after the author of the original Bitcoin whitepaper, this is a unit of Bitcoin... 0.00000001 of a Bitcoin!

- Bitcoin halving: An event is when the reward for mining bitcoin transactions is cut in half. Previous halvings have correlated with intense boom and bust cycles that have ended with higher prices than prior to the event.

- Block: A collection of Bitcoin transactions that have occurred during a period (typically about 10 minutes). If the blockchain is thought of as a ledger book, a block is like one page from the book.

- Address: A string of letters and numbers from which bitcoins can be sent to and from. A bitcoin address can be shared publicly, and like sending a message to an email address, a bitcoin address can be provided to others that wish to send you bitcoin.

- Ledger: A physical or electronic logbook containing a list of transactions and balances typically involving financial accounts. The Bitcoin blockchain is the first distributed, decentralized, public ledger.

- Peer-to-Peer: A type of network where participants communicate directly with each other rather than through a centralized server. The Bitcoin network is peer-to-peer.

- Private Key: A string of letters and numbers that can be used to spend bitcoins associated with a specific Bitcoin address.

- Public Key: A string of letters and numbers that is derived from a private key. A public key allows one to receive bitcoins.

- QR Code: A digital representation of a bitcoin public or private key that is easy to scan by digital cameras. QR codes are similar to barcodes found on physical products in that they are a machine-friendly way to embody a piece of data.

- Signature: A portion of a Bitcoin transaction authenticating that the private key owner has approved the transaction.

- Transaction: An entry in the blockchain that describes a transfer of bitcoins from one address to another. Bitcoin transactions may contain several inputs and outputs.

- Cryptography: In the context of Bitcoin, cryptography is the use of mathematics to secure information. Cryptography is used to create and secure wallets, sign transactions, and verify the blockchain.

- Crypto tokens: Unlike digital coins, crypto tokens are created on existing blockchains. For example, tokens that are built on the Ethereum platform are known as ERC-20 tokens. Tokens can be either fungible or non-fungible tokens (NFTs).

- SHA-256: The specific hash function used in the mining process to secure bitcoin transactions.

- Decentralized: Without a central authority or controlling party. Bitcoin is a decentralized network since no company, government, or individual is in control of it.

- Distributed: A distributed network is designed to have no central server or entity that others must connect to. Instead, network participants connect directly to each other. Bitcoin is a distributed network.

- Miners: Network users who donate their time and computing power to help with encrypting and verifying transactions.

- Node: A participant in the Bitcoin network. Nodes share a copy of the blockchain and relay new transactions to other nodes.`

- M of N: The number of cosigners that must provide signatures (M) out of the total number of cosigners (N) for a multi-signature bitcoin transaction to take place. A typical M of N value is "2 of

3," meaning two of the three cosigners' signatures are required.

- Multi-Signature: Also called multisig. A bitcoin transaction requires signatures from multiple parties before it can be executed. Coinbase multi-sig vaults use this type of technology.

- Confirmations: A bitcoin transaction is considered unconfirmed until it has been included in a block on the blockchain, at which point it has one confirmation. Each additional block is another confirmation. Coinbase requires three confirmations to consider a bitcoin transaction final.

- Cosigner: An additional person or entity that has partial control over a Bitcoin wallet.

- Proof of Work: A piece of data that requires a significant amount of computation to generate but requires a minimal amount of computation to be verified as being correct. Bitcoin uses proof of work to generate new blocks.

- Protocol: The official rules that dictate how participants on a network must communicate. Bitcoin's protocol specifies how each node connects with the others, how many bitcoins will exist at any point in time and defines other aspects of the network.

- Transaction: An entry in the blockchain that describes a transfer of bitcoins from one address to another. Bitcoin transactions may contain several inputs and outputs.

- Transaction Fee: Also known as a "miner's" fee, a transaction fee is an amount of bitcoin included in each transaction that miners collect. This is to encourage miners to add the transaction to a block. A typical bitcoin fee amount is 0.0001 BTC.

- Exchanges: Businesses that buy and sell cryptocurrencies. Originally, they connected buyers with sellers, but most these days seem to let you deal with them directly for a faster turnaround

- Cold Wallet: A Bitcoin wallet that is in cold storage (not connected to the internet). Cold storage lets you keep Bitcoin entirely offline

- Hot Wallet: A Bitcoin wallet that resides on a device that is connected to the internet. A wallet installed on a desktop computer or smartphone is usually a hot wallet.

- Vault: A type of Bitcoin wallet provided by Coinbase. Vault accounts add additional time-lock and security measures to protect your funds.

- Wallet: A collection of Bitcoin private keys used to spend bitcoins.

CHAPTER 2

HOW THE BITCOIN LANDSCAPE HAS EVOLVED

To say the Bitcoin landscape has changed over the past decade is the understatement of the century (actually the millennium). At some levels, the story of Bitcoin's evolution from 2009 to 2021 (and beyond) reminds me of the childhood story of the ugly duckling turning into a swan. Of course, Bitcoin's metamorphosis into the proverbial swan has permanently altered the world of finance, politics, economics, and perhaps how we interact with the world in the near future.

2.1: How It Started

Like so many great things in life, Bitcoin started not with a bang but a whimper. In October 2008, the mythical Satoshi Nakamoto posted a white paper titled Bitcoin: A Peer-to-Peer Electronic Cash System on a cryptography mailing list. While the concept of Bitcoin was introduced in the white paper, Bitcoins only became a reality in 2009 when an open-source software was released in conjunction with other coders and software developers. The open-source software provides an autonomous platform that is 'mined' by people seeking Bitcoins in a lottery-based system. Unlike normal centralised or fiat currencies that we use in our day-to-day lives whose supply is controlled by central banks, only 21 million Bitcoins exist, of which 18.5 million have been mined as of 2021. So Bitcoins are limited and rapidly running out (certainly running out faster than oil). One of the earliest crypto-enthusiasts was Hal Finney, a console game developer who offered to mine ten original bitcoins from block 70, which Nakamoto sent over as a test. Satoshi Nakamoto's identity is unknown (although Nakamoto is estimated to hold about a million Bitcoins). So despite his massive Bitcoin holdings, Nakamoto is not in-charge of Bitcoins. While no centralised authorities are running the show, its governance is carried out through a set of verification rules covering everything from data structures to transaction verification. The Bitcoin transactions are verified via mining (which does not involve swinging an axe) by solving complex computational puzzles to maintain the ledger of transactions upon which Bitcoin is based. However, given the increasing complexity of these puzzles, it's no longer feasible for individuals to try and mine on their personal computers (more of this in section 2.2.1). Bitcoins were officially in business (although throughout 2009, they were not used for financial transactions).

2.1.1 Jittery Beginnings (And a Multi-Million Dollar Pizza)

For a very long time, bitcoins were used by a limited number of people, a small dedicated community of cryptographers with precious little mainstream interest. One of the earliest known bitcoin transactions was for pizza. Specifically, two pizzas from Papa John's. The pizza (and bitcoin aficionado) was Laszlo Hanyecz, who paid 10,000 Bitcoins for the pizzas. You read that right; 10,000 bitcoins which were worth around $80 million in 2018. However, in 2010, this was one of the first examples of Bitcoins being used to carry out a transaction (until this point, Bitcoins had only been mined, never formally traded). Don't we all wish we could go back to 2010?

Bitcoin quickly went from being a fringe item to a facilitator of vice and crimes (and got a fair bit of notoriety in the process) courtesy of the Silk Road saga. Silk Road was an online black market where buyers and sellers could trade illegal or unethical items, including drugs, anonymously via cryptocurrency transactions. Founded by Ross William Ulbricht (who is now serving a life term in the US) in 2011, it was the first darknet marketplace. The FBI shut it down in 2013 and seized more than 144,000 bitcoins. This was one of the first occasions when Bitcoin made mainstream news and entered the public consciousness (arguably, not in a pleasant way). Perhaps it was Bitcoin's infamous Silk Road connection that prompted J.P. Morgan's head honcho to label Bitcoins as being an entity that was only used by drug traffickers, criminals, and people living in North Korea (I am not entirely sure what was the logic behind conflating millions of North Koreans with drug traffickers). On an unrelated note, a cargo ship owned by JPMorgan Chase was seized by the US with 20 tons of cocaine in 2019.

2.2 How It's Going

Quite briefly, very well, and very volatile.

2.2.1 Bitcoin Mining Is Increasingly Out Of the Reach of Solo Miners

As of 2021, Bitcoin mining is no longer feasible for solo miners. Since 2013, application-specific integrated circuit (ASIC) miners have dominated the bitcoin mining space (Bitmain's AntMiner S19 Pro, S19, and T19 are arguably the most efficient Bitcoin miners available). Additionally, one would need to be part of a mining pool to make any tangible gains, and keeping an eye on the electricity costs is a must. There are many other books out there that cover the nitty-gritty of Bitcoin mining, so this is not something I am going to cover in this book. According to the research done by Stoll et al. 1., ASIC-driven Bitcoin mining is increasingly being concentrated in places that have low electricity costs, including Venezuela, Russia, and China.

Figure 2: Spatial Distribution of Bitman ASIC Devices 1

So outside of these locations, there is a strong chance the electricity and equipment costs could eat into the potential Bitcoin mining profits. Further, bitcoin mining is subject to newer regulatory oversight and taxation. This is worth bearing in mind for any newbie miner. For those starting in the Bitcoin world, purchasing and trading Bitcoins (and related assets) is a much more feasible pathway to gaining exposure to this sector. Hence, Bitcoin investment strategies form the crux of this book.

2.2.2 Volatile Price Action

April 13 is a historical date for many reasons. Now adding to the notoriety of April 13 is Bitcoin; on this day in 2021, Bitcoin touched its all-time high price of $64,888. Quite a jump from being $9000 in March 2020. However, the Bitcoin price action started on a more damp note. While Bitcoin started at $0 in 2009, it started trading from around $0.0008 to $0.08 per coin in July 2010 (where is that time machine when I need it??!!!). The highest price it achieved was $0.39 in 2010 (prices remained firmly below $1). See figure 3.

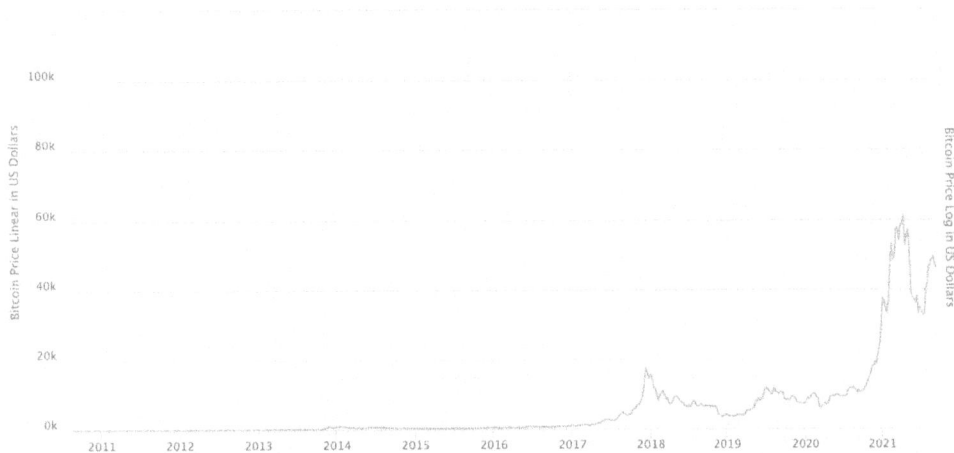

Figure 3: Bitcoin Price Action (Aug 2010-Sept 14, 2021). Data was taken from:
https://www.statista.com/statistics/326707/bitcoin-price-index/

If Bitcoin's price action is not one blessed roller coaster, I don't know what is. Bitcoin's price jumped from $1 in April 2011 to $32 in June 2021. But the 3200% gain did not last for long, and bitcoin prices fell back to $2 in November 2011. While trading at around $13 in 2013, Bitcoin encountered not one but two 'bubbles' in terms of two bullish runs followed by crashes. In April 2013 alone, Bitcoin crossed $200 and fell back below $70. Prices again climbed up, and by October, Bitcoin was trading around $123, and the price finally crossed $1000 in December 2013, although Bitcoin's membership of the $1000+ club was relatively short-lived. 2017 was another year of Bitcoin price milestones; from hovering near $1000 in March 2017, Bitcoin climbed to $20,000+ by December 2017. While Bitcoin started attracting mainstream attention, its price moved sideways for the next two years. While it crossed $10,000 again in 2019, Bitcoin ended 2019 in the $7000 range. However, the global COVID pandemic was going to change all that. But before that, here is a brief chart that shows the price corrections from 2012-2018:

Correction start date	Correction end date	# Days in correction	Bitcoin high price $	Bitcoin low price $	Decline %	Decline $
12 Jan 2012	27 Jan 2012	16	7.38	3.80	-49%	3.58
17 Aug 2012	19 Aug 2012	3	16.41	7.10	-57%	9.31
6 Mar 2013	7 Mar 2013	2	49.17	33.00	-33%	16.17
21 Mar 2013	23 Mar 2013	3	76.91	50.09	-35%	26.82
10 Apr 2013	12 Apr 2013	3	259.34	45.00	-83%	214.34
19 Nov 2013	19 Nov 2013	1	755.00	378.00	-50%	377.00
30 Nov 2013	14 Jan 2015	411	1,163.00	152.40	-87%	1,010.60
10 Mar 2017	25 Mar 2017	16	1,350.00	891.33	-34%	458.67
25 May 2017	27 May 2017	3	2,760.10	1,850.00	-33%	910.10
12 Jun 2017	16 Jul 2017	35	2,980.00	1,830.00	-39%	1,150.00
2 Sep 2017	15 Sep 2017	14	4,979.90	2,972.01	-40%	2,007.89
8 Nov 2017	12 Nov 2017	5	7,888.00	5,555.55	-30%	2,332.45
17 Dec 2017	2 Feb 2018	48	19,666.00	8,094.80	-59%	11,571.20
29 Aug 2018	8 Dec 2018	100	7,091.71	3,392.70	-48%	3,699.01

Figure 4: Historical Bitcoin (BTC) Market Corrections (Taskinsoy 2018)

Historically, BTC markets have had market corrections of more than 50% (and around 80%+ in 2015) on several occasions. On September 9, 2020, Bitcoin crossed $10,000 and later on in the year proceeded to touch all-time highs and finally, for the first time, surpassed $40,000 in January 2021. In hindsight, such a price progression makes sense as the COVID 19 pandemic and ensuing economic upheaval forced many people to see bitcoin as a hedge and store of value, accelerating its mainstream penetration. While many experts are debating whether Bitcoin can touch $100,000 (and indeed Cathie Woods of ARK Investments predicts a price increase to $500,000), it's worth bearing in mind that Bitcoin is a relatively new entrant to the $10,000+ club and has dropped out of this coveted club on quite a few occasions. Given the Bitcoin price volatility, sharp price declines are entirely possible, and late entrants need to brace themselves for potential mega pullbacks.

2.2.3 Increasing Mainstream Adoption (and Regulation Attempts)

2021 proved to be a watershed year for Bitcoins (and other cryptocurrencies). Bitcoin has officially entered the mainstream consciousness, with mainstream adoption and governmental attempts to regulate the crypto space happening in tandem. In the earlier part of 2021, Elon Musk made massive waves in the bitcoin world by investing in Bitcoins and agreeing to accept Bitcoins as payment for Teslas and then walking back on the payment acceptance in May 2021 (causing a massive drop in Bitcoin prices). Elon Musk's interventions aside, as of 2021, JP Morgan has started giving its wealth management clients access to half a dozen crypto funds. This change in stance from 2017 is a typical example of how far Bitcoin has come and its increasing mainstream acceptance and growing institutional support. Wall Street's attempts to launch a Bitcoin ETF has gained renewed vigour (although attempts have been made since 2009, this fresh push indicates a new enthusiasm about the Bitcoin space). In the meantime, many big investment banks are expanding their crypto services; as of March 2021, Morgan Stanley has proposed to let its wealthier clients choose three Bitcoin funds for more aggressive investments. As of 2021, Paypal has also started rolling out its cryptocurrency service. Its newly launched UK service will allow users to buy and sell bitcoins (along with some other select cryptocurrencies) for a minimum of £1. The UK's Post Office also plans to offer cryptocurrency investments to its customers. Apart from increasing institutional acceptance, Bitcoin is seeing increasing governmental acceptance (and attempts to regulate it).

El Salvador has become the first country globally to adopt Bitcoin as a legal tender by passing the Bitcoin Law (on June 8, 2021) and through its subsequent purchase of 400 bitcoins. While this step has been hailed as revolutionary, the actual rollout resulted in difficulties causing Bitcoin prices to plummet unexpectedly on September 8, 2021. Like many other Latin American countries that rely on remittances, Bitcoin adoption of El-Salvador's population ranges from 10%-20%. However, El-Salvador is a test case of how crypto adoption can be influenced by active government intervention. Given the increasing governmental interest in Bitcoin adoption and regulation (as of September 2021, governments of Ukraine and Panama have introduced legislative bills to regulate Bitcoin adoption). Banco Central de Cuba (BCC), Cuba's central bank, now permits cryptocurrencies like Bitcoin (BTC) as a payment method in the country. As of October 2021, Brazilians will buy houses, cars, and McDonald's with Bitcoins.

However, anyone observing the crypto space will know that not all governmental intervention is Bitcoin-friendly. In 2021, China launched a crackdown on cryptocurrencies by targeting miners and imposing curbs on crypto banking services and trading while pushing for the adoption of digital yuan. As of Sept 24, 2021, China has rendered all crypto coin transactions illegal. China had previously launched a Bitcoin crackdown in 2017 when it shut down exchanges and banned initial coin offerings (ICOs). India, another billion-dollar population country, is also trying to regulate the crypto space. As of 2021, US Treasury Secretary Janet Yellen has called for increased regulation of the crypto space and the popular crypto exchange. As of September 2021, Coinbase was sued by the US's Security and Exchange Commission (SEC). So as of 2021, it does seem the Holy Trinity of three major countries- India, China, and the US have a bee in their bonnet about Bitcoins. Going forward, this could potentially increase the Bitcoin price action volatility, but it is too early to speculate if these measures could do any lasting damage to the crypto space. After all, the great philosopher Victor Hugo once said, "Nothing is more powerful than an idea whose time has come."

I have presented a brief synopsis of the happenings in the world of Bitcoins from its inception to 2021 with the view of illustrating just one key point- Bitcoin has arrived. From being a non-entity a few years ago, it is increasingly finding itself in some exciting tug-of-war situations. As new entrants, it is worth bearing in mind that these tugs-of-war could be part of the crypto space in the foreseeable future, adding to the volatility of an already volatile asset. This calls for clear-cut strategies so as not to be swayed by market sentiment and treat Bitcoins like any other medium-to-long-term investment strategy. As I pointed out before, my book is not a get-rich-quick strategy hack, and the focus is to help develop medium-to-long-term investment strategies. In the meantime, love it or hate it, you can't ignore Bitcoin.

2.2.4 Emissions Implications

After eagerly embracing Bitcoin at the start of 2021, on May 12, 2021, Elon Musk sent the Bitcoin world (and prices) into a tizzy by stating that Tesla would not accept bitcoins as payment over emission concerns. The prices fell from $52,000 to $48,000. Elon Musk did hit the nail on the head when he spoke up about Bitcoin's emission impacts (although I personally doubt he was solely motivated by environmental concerns, and I find it very hard to believe that he was unaware of the Bitcoin mining emissions when he first made a foray into the Bitcoin world and sent the prices soaring). However, as Bitcoin gains more traction, so will the discussions around emissions implications of mining Bitcoins (and other cryptocurrencies). According to the Cambridge Bitcoin Electricity Consumption Index (CBECI), the source quoted by Musk in his infamous tweet, the energy usage for Bitcoin mining has been steadily rising (see figure 4). Bitcoins electricity consumption adds about 40 million tons of carbon dioxide to the atmosphere a year.

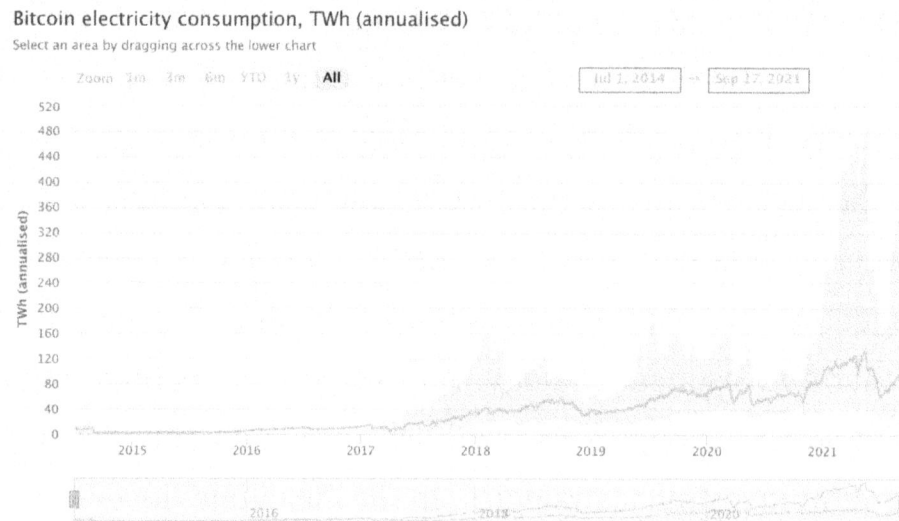

Bitcoin electricity consumption, TWh (annualised)
Select an area by dragging across the lower chart

Figure 5: Bitcoin Electricity Consumption from 2014-2021 (Source: https://cbeci.org/).

A substantial portion of this electricity comes from fossil fuels, giving Bitcoin a high carbon footprint. According to a study by Stoll et al. (2019) [1], published in the scientific journal Joule, Bitcoin production approximately generates between 22 and 22.9 million metric tons of carbon dioxide emissions a year, equivalent to the levels produced by Jordan and Sri Lanka. The discussion around Bitcoin's energy consumption and carbon footprint will not go away any time soon. Needless to say, this issue will add further volatility to an already volatile asset. However, with volatility comes opportunity. The mainstreaming of Bitcoins could give a boost to the renewables sector. In fact, Innovation seems underway. Bill Spence, a former oil industry engineer's enterprise, the Scrubgrass Generating power plant uses discarded bituminous garbage ('gob') to power energy-hungry computers that validate the Bitcoin transactions 2. While the scalability and the large-scale adaptability of such measures remain to be seen, the use of waste and renewables for crypto mining could open new avenues for inventors and investors. I will discuss the possible pathways to profiting from such emerging Bitcoin-related trends in Chapter 7.

CHAPTER 3

THE ART AND SCIENCE OF BUYING (AND STORING) BITCOINS

Now, the upshot of this chapter, and indeed of this book, is that we will not mine Bitcoins and other cryptocurrencies computationally. However, having access to heavy-duty computational resources is not the only way to obtain Bitcoins; indeed, you can exchange Bitcoins (and other cryptocurrencies) on crypto exchanges. Buying cryptocurrencies on a specialised exchange is no different from buying your favourite stock or ETF on the stock exchange. And you certainly don't need $50,000 to buy a Bitcoin. Most crypto exchanges allow users to buy fractional units (in this chapter, I will cover how the ability to do so is a game-changer for small investors). Since crypto-assets exist only in the digital world, these have to be stored in special digital wallets. In principle, they are the digital versions of the wallets we use in real life to carry about our money. These crypto-wallets can exist online or offline (as cold wallets). It is essential to be aware of all these concepts before starting one's crypto journey. In this chapter, I will first start by covering the basic nuts and bolts you need to be aware of (the different exchanges and apps you can use to buy cryptocurrencies, one app to avoid if you are British, the different kinds of wallets) moving onto the actual Bitcoin accumulation strategies.

3.1 Where to Buy Bitcoins (and Other Cryptos)?

In most countries, Bitcoins can be bought on crypto exchanges. Some of the most common bitcoin exchanges include Binance, Coinbase, Kraken, Gemini, Crypto.com, Bitstamp, to name a few which allow both trading and custodial services (that is, you can buy and sell your crypto assets through these exchanges and store them with these providers as well). However, crypto exchange availability may vary by country. For instance, Currency.com, Rain, and Luno are popular in Africa, West Asia, and parts of SE Asia. It's worth cross-checking which ones are available in your jurisdiction. But almost all crypto exchanges can be obtained via the Apple App Store or Google Play, enabling you to access these crypto exchanges via your smart devices. This can be both a boon and a curse (I will discuss this later). However, for those in the UK, USA, and other Western countries, the most common crypto exchanges to buy Bitcoin (and other digital assets) include:

3.1.1 Coinbase

Coinbase is one of the most popular crypto exchanges in the US. It's available in more than 100 countries, and wherever you live, the chances are that you can obtain Coinbase. It has a vast choice of cryptocurrencies (although some of the newer projects turn up on Binance well before they do on Coinbase). Essentially Coinbase allows the users to buy the most popular currencies, and for the newer and underrated ones, Binance is your friend. It had a successful IPO in April 2021. While it has a Pro version available (which allows crypto trading), the standard version is sufficient for those of you who are starting out or indeed have been buying cryptos for a while. I am an avid Coinbase user myself (however, I am not affiliated with them in shape or form). I think it has a very intuitive feel, making it quite user-friendly, especially for newbies.

Further, unlike Binance and Kraken that require higher minimum transactions, you can buy fractional crypto for a minimum of £2. Additionally, you can set up an autosave to buy cryptos for a given amount weekly. This form of investing is known as dollar-cost-averaging and can go a long way in building one's portfolio (I will discuss the nitty-gritty in chapter 4). You can also exchange one crypto for another. So if one of your smaller alt-coins has a sharp price increase, you could swap some of those profits for a BTC fraction without converting to fiat money. Coinbase offers biometric security, two-step verification, and insurance in case there is a breach at Coinbase. However, this insurance is not valid if you perform any act of carelessness. And it is not just retail investors like me who love Coinbase; it is becoming rather popular with institutional investors. Genesis Trading, which the Grayscale Bitcoin Trust uses for Bitcoin procurement, uses the Coinbase OTC ("Over-the-Counter ") desk for executing their trades. Other sizeable institutional Bitcoin investors such as Ruffer Investment Management have also used Coinbase for their BTC purchases. However, there is a slightly disconcerting note. In October 2021, it was revealed that between March and May 20th, 2021, a threat actor stole cryptocurrency from at least 6,000 customers after using a vulnerability to bypass the company's SMS multi-factor authentication security feature. Coinbase has reimbursed the affected parties, and I was personally not affected by this breach. While Coinbase is still a solid choice for procuring crypto assets, these incidents point to the importance of storing your cryptos offline (I will discuss this in section 3.3).

3.1.2 Binance

Binance has both a Lite and a Pro version, and the former is sufficient for those starting out. It is the world's largest crypto exchange (by trading volume). Frankly, it's the crypto exchange to go-to for all the latest crypto coins (as they are usually listed on Binance before other crypto exchanges). While Binance has its origins in China, it is now based out of Japan. Strictly in terms of usage, Binance has a clunkier interface than Coinbase, and in the UK, you have to spend a minimum of £15 per transaction. There are no autosaves available (not at least in the Lite version). However, features and usability are not the only factors to consider if planning to use Binance. In 2021 Binance was rocked by a series of regulatory issues which potential users must bear in mind. For instance, Britain's financial regulator has banned Binance because it doesn't have any approval in writing. However, this does not mean that local investors in the UK can't trade. As of Oct 2021, UK users have typically used their Binance accounts (both the Lite and Standard versions). India's Enforcement Directorate (ED), the agency responsible for enforcing economic laws and fighting financial crime, goes after WazirX (Binance's Indian subsidiary) after allegedly allowing users to transact digital currencies without proper documentation. This, according to the ED, is a violation of the nation's Foreign Exchange Management Act (FEMA), and WazirX has been asked to explain $258.3 million worth of transactions (as of July 21, 2021). In July 2021, Binance ceased its operations in Ontario (Canada) in the face of the threat of regulatory sanctions by the Ontario Securities Commission (OSC). If you are new to the world of cryptocurrencies, I can suggest focussing on other exchanges till there is more clarity.

3.1.3 Kraken

While Kraken is not as intuitive as Coinbase, it is undoubtedly not as clunky as Binance. Moreso, you can buy cryptocurrency using Apple Pay which makes it quite convenient. However, the minimum transaction value is around £10. Plus, it has good security features (as of 2021, it is yet to be hacked and has a decade-long track record) and is based in the US. It has a wide selection of coins to choose from. The platform also offers staking/loaning capabilities and access margin (but I strongly recommend gaining experience before using these advanced features). However, one of its most convenient features is that it lets you see the biggest gainers and losers in the past 24 hrs at a glance.

3.1.4 Gemini

This is a crypto exchange based in the US (and is available in all US states). It launched in 2015 and offered fewer crypto assets than other common exchanges such as Kraken or Coinbase. However, they have many different functionalities, including Gemini Earn, Gemini Pay, and Gemini Wallet, which offer more advanced capabilities such as earning interest on one's crypto assets. The interest varies from 2% to 7.4% annual interest and is paid in the allocated cryptocurrency. Now more excitingly, as of the summer of 2021, Gemini offers a bitcoin-backed Mastercard. The card does not give out points or cashback. Instead, it provides real-time rewards in the form of more than 30 different cryptocurrencies a cardholder can pick from, including bitcoin, ether, or Litecoin, and earn back 3%. This offering had quite a long waiting list, so I could not lay my hands on it, but for me, this is another example of mainstreaming bitcoins (and other cryptos) and allowing people to benefit tangibly.

3.1.5 KuCoin

While KuCoin is not registered in the US, it's still an attractive platform for more experienced users, especially those looking to trade or lend out their cryptos for interest (I will cover crypto lending further in this book). Its transaction charges are 0.1%, making it attractive for frequent users. However, the interface is known to be clunkier than Binance's. So if it's the ease of use you are looking for as a beginner, it may be worth avoiding KuCoin while you get comfortable with the crypto space.

3.1.6 CEX.io

This is a London-based crypto exchange with a pretty strong security record. It claims not to have lost any client funds. Further, it is registered with FinCEN in the United States and as a Money Services Businesses in the United Kingdom. Cex.io also received the second level certificate of the Payment Card Industry Security Standard. However, it has relatively higher brokerage fees (and if you don't want to switch to the trading version, this is worth remembering). For me, the security features and certifications are assuring. Further, you can connect your bank account to buy cryptos.

3.1.7 FTX

FTX generated a bit of a buzz when it decided to shift its headquarters from Hong Kong to the Bahamas in the wake of China's latest cryptocurrency ban. To be very fair, this is a platform better suited for more experienced traders as it allows for futures trading and access to leveraged tokens. It has also ventured into the non-fungible token (NFT) domain, making it an all-rounder compared to vanilla crypto exchanges such as Coinbase. It does have a pretty decent price alert system, so those looking for price alerts may want to consider this.

3.1.8 Crypto.com:

To be very fair, this was one of the first crypto exchanges I latched onto, and I found it to be a bit overwhelming. It is a very feature-rich crypto exchange (which paradoxically may intimidate one at the onset) with a healthy selection of currencies. It does have higher monetary requirements for withdrawal and other activities such as auto-transactions, and users have struggled to withdraw monies to their GBP accounts. But it offers many features (which I will expand on further in the book) that make it worth grappling with.

3.1.9 Uphold:

Uphold is a cloud-based financial service platform available on iOS and Android devices (https://uphold.com/en-gb) that enables individuals to move securely, convert, hold and transact in various financial assets. Although it is commonly associated with Bitcoin and other cryptocurrencies, it also trades traditional assets such as fiat currencies/forex and gold. As of October 2021, Uphold is available in the USA, UK, most European countries, and India. So Uphold members - in any market - can instantly send money or make payments to anyone in India, redeemable directly through any Indian bank. As for cryptocurrencies, you can buy and sell most cryptocurrencies, including Bitcoin. There are dedicated wallets for Bitcoin and Ethereum, along with a few more cryptocurrencies. Additionally, the app allows investment in forex pairs and gold. Members from 174+ countries can start saving long-term with as little as $5.

I have just highlighted some of the most common crypto exchanges around and which are available in most countries. Another crypto solution, Caspian Tech (https://caspian.tech/), lets users access a number of crypto exchanges straight from one platform. Another desktop and mobile-based tracker is the Delta investment Tracker (https://delta.app/en) provided by the social trading platform eToro (more on this in chapter 6). It allows users to track their crypto portfolios (across multiple crypto exchanges) along with their stock portfolios. To be very fair, I am an avid eToro user, and I feel Delta is a better (and more comprehensive) tracking option.

Most of these crypto exchanges are required to perform some kind of KYC (know your customer) due diligence. This means in order to use these crypto exchanges (or at least in order to get full access), you have to provide personal details such as name, date of birth, proof of identification such as your passport, along with providing bank account details. One important thing I discovered (somewhat painfully) is that the name you register on the app must match your bank account name. And this brings me to a rather unfortunate experience I had with a UK crypto app: Mode App, which I tell all my friends to avoid.

WHY I WOULD AVOID THE MODE APP FOR BITCOIN PURCHASES

My initial foray into the world of Bitcoins started with the Mode app. I don't mind admitting I was a complete newbie at that point, so I am in part answerable for the mess I found myself in. However, I do Mode App was less than scrupulous in their dealings, so I feel this one is worth skipping. As it happened, I deposited £50 (the minimum balance requirement) using a bank account that went by the name M Singh while I was registered as Minerva Singh on the app. So the names did not match and indeed, as I discovered later that a name mismatch like this can be problematic across other apps too.

However, what got my goat is that while the names did not match, they still accepted my deposit of £50 but did not let me buy Bitcoins with it. So if the name issue is such a big thing for them, they should not have accepted my deposit, and frankly, users should be made aware of this issue right at the onset. I contacted them via Instagram, email and the App store. No avail. Neither was my money returned, nor could I buy any Bitcoins. Then one fine day, I got an email from them telling me they had shut my account. And no, my £50 were never returned to me. While I have no doubts they must have taken legal precautions to justify their conduct under their Terms and Conditions, I found their conduct to be deceitful. The way I see it, what would have happened if I had put £5000 into the app? I have no doubts they would have digested that too without burping. However, thankfully there are many professional and contentious service providers out there.

Of course, some exchanges do not need this information for people who are unable or unwilling to go through the KYC procedures. Peer-to-peer exchanges such as Bisq, Bitquick, Paxful, and Local Bitcoins also exist, allowing for buying and selling bitcoins for fiat currency using peer-to-peer networks and do not require any registration. Scotland-based crypto-custodian Zumo has moved beyond traditional bank account linkages and now supports Modulr's Open Banking enabled top-ups. I have not personally used any of these, so I cannot comment on how good or bad these are.

3.2 Non-Crypto Exchange Apps To Buy Bitcoins

Other apps are not typical crypto exchanges, but they do let you buy and store cryptocurrencies. These include:

3.2.1 Revolut

This, for me, is the ultimate financial multi-planning app and a great all-purpose solution to both saving and spending. This banking app lets you manage your money online and comes with a card for spending. However, it is still way ahead of the curve than other banking apps such as Starling. I will not wax lyrical about the numerous features of Revolut (and why it's a must-have for budgeting). Instead, cutting to the chase, this banking app, unlike others, allows you to buy and store cryptocurrencies.

Additionally, you can set up autosaves to buy your favourite cryptos (including Bitcoins) at regular intervals. I found this app to be a good way of growing crypto stockpiles while balancing the household books. Over the past few months, the app has expanded in terms of its crypto offerings.

3.2.2 Ziglu

Ziglu is a UK-based app, open to UK residents over the age of 18. In addition to letting people buy Bitcoins and other cryptocurrencies from £1. Additionally, Ziglu has a referral program that lets you earn a fee every time you refer someone. The app provides a card, and you can send and receive both cash and crypto. This duality of supporting cash and crypto also extends to its Sterling Boost and Bitcoin Boost accounts, which offer up to 5% interest on cash and crypto deposits. However, in my experience, their customer service does leave a lot to be desired. If you get locked out of your account as I did, don't expect a response. So it's an innovative app, but I don't feel comfortable recommending this to my friends and family.

3.2.3 Paypal UK

Last but not least, you can now buy and hold cryptocurrencies such as

Bitcoin on your personal Paypal account in the UK. Note: you cannot buy and hold Bitcoins on your business Paypal account. Further, as of October 2021, PayPal's cryptocurrency service is not regulated by the UK Financial Conduct Authority or the Luxembourg Commission De Surveillance Du Secteur Financier. Venmo, the mobile payment service owned by PayPal, enabled the sale and purchase through its functionality in April 2021.

3.2.4 Robinhood

While Robinhood ($HOOD) is not yet available in the UK, 2020-21 was its coming of age time. Robinhood is a financial services firm (that was publicly listed earlier in 2021) that provides commission-free stock trading and investing. The 2020 COVID-19 saw a large number of retail traders gravitate to trading apps, with Robinhood leading the pack. In early 2021, Robinhood (indirectly) helped fuel the meme stock mania. As of September 2021, Robinhood is planning to launch its crypto wallet with the view of letting its users buy Bitcoin through the platform. Like stocks, the sale and purchase of bitcoins are commission-free. Through the proposed wallet, users will be able to purchase, send and receive Bitcoins.

3.2.5 Cash App

Square's Cash App was an early Bitcoin adapter when it enabled users to trade Bitcoins through its interface back in 2017. This has worked well to Square's advantage (more details in chapter 7). Through the app, you can buy both Bitcoins and stocks for as little as $1.Cash App is PCI Data Security Standard (PCI-DSS) Level 1 compliant. This keeps the user payment information encrypted and sent securely to the app servers whether one is using public or private Wi-Fi or data services such as 3G,

4G, and EDGE.

3.3 Store Your Bitcoins Offline (Cold Wallets)

Over the past few years, there have been many incidences of crypto exchanges being hacked and having their cryptos stolen. What happened to Coinbase in the summer of 2021 is just one example of hackers gaining access to online or hot wallets. I could write a separate book dedicated to incidents of hot wallet hacking. But the bottom line is that for all the security protocols crypto exchanges follow, hot wallets (which are available as online, digital and software wallets) remain vulnerable to hacking. This is why those planning to make substantial crypto investments need to consider using hardware or offline/cold wallets. Hardware wallets are certainly not as convenient to use as the internet-connected hot wallets, but they offer unparalleled security as they store private keys offline. Most hardware wallets are the size of a pen drive, and you need to plug them into your computer to transfer your bitcoins (and other cryptos such as Ethereum) the way you would transfer documents or files from your hard drive to a USB. Of course, setting up hardware wallets is more complicated than that, and you do have to note the seed phrase generated. Without that, you don't get access to your bitcoins- EVER. Some of the best hardware wallets out there are:

3.3.1 Ledger Nano X:

Ledger employs a custom-built OS (BOLOS) and CC EAL5+ certified Secure Element (SE) chip. The device's security has also been audited and verified by ANSSI, the French national cybersecurity agency. It's worth around $119, and I could not find it on Amazon UK. It is available from the company's UK website for about £109. It has a cheaper cousin, **Ledger Nano S**, priced around £54. However, Ledger Nano X can store a greater range of assets and allows you to manage your portfolio on the go by linking the device to the smartphone app via Bluetooth. Further, these wallets allow connectivity with crypto exchanges Coinify and Changelly and DeFi protocol Compound to allow users to grow their crypto assets while storing them in hardware wallets. However, the company did suffer from a data breach. While this did not jeopardize the security of the actual wallets, this is a point worth bearing in mind.

3.3.2 Trezor Model T

Created by SatoshiLabs in 2014, this is the older hardware wallet in circulation. It allows users to store more than 1600 different kinds of crypto assets. It has a built-in touch screen to enable you to enter the PIN and passphrase on the device itself. Setting it up for the first time can be complicated and counter-intuitive. Still, this hardware wallet offers the functionality of directly buying and storing the cryptos within the cold storage wallet itself. Its poorer cousin, Trezor Model One, is limited in its choice of supported cryptocurrencies.

3.3.3 Secu X W 20

This, too, boasts of military-grade hardware and the ability to support most major cryptos. It is undoubtedly bigger than Trezor, and its larger touch screen makes it user-friendly. It can be connected both to computers and mobile devices via WiFi or Bluetooth. It claims to provide on-screen verification of addresses to provide malware protection from fund tampering. It has been listed at around £89 on Amazon UK.

3.3.4 D'CENT Biometric Wallet

As the name suggests, this hardware wallet provides biometric verification, which the other three mentioned here don't. It features a certified Secure chip(EAL5+) and a built-in Fingerprint sensor for highly secured transactions, which can be enabled via iOS or Android apps by simply providing one's fingerprints. I do find this quite innovative since fingerprints are unique to every person. It has been listed at around £102 on Amazon UK.

The hacker-proof nature of these hardware wallets also creates another set of problems, mainly in the form of lost passwords and seed phrases (as Albert Einstein famously remarked, human stupidity is infinite). A case in point is the German-born programmer Stefan Thomas whose lost password left him unable to access more than 7000 Bitcoins stored on his hardware wallet (he was essentially locked out of a $200 million+ fortune). These cases are not all that rare. New York Times reported a nugget of information from the cryptocurrency data firm Chainalysis. Of the existing 18.5 million Bitcoin, around 20 per cent — currently worth around $140 billion — appear to be in lost or otherwise stranded wallets. This is quite a whopping amount, so if you decide to store your stash in a cold wallet, please take steps to ensure you are not left out in the cold.

3.4 Middle of the Path Solutions

If you are dissatisfied with the security offered by crypto exchanges but don't want to move your cryptos offline, there are some middle of path solutions for you to consider. While desktop and mobile wallets are hot wallets, they still offer peace of mind by letting you move your cryptos off the crypto exchanges. And they remain a couple of clicks away for your convenience. Some of the most common desktop and mobile wallet app solutions include:

3.4.1 Exodus

It's a befitting Biblical name for a desktop-based solution that offers pretty powerful capabilities, especially for those starting in the crypto world. While it originally had a desktop-only version, it now offers iOS and Android apps, making it a desktop and mobile wallet. It has a robust, beginner-friendly user interface (UI) which I have no doubts will make many beginners happy. It is suitable for exchanging small amounts of cryptos. However, it should be borne in mind that the ability to set custom fees is currently restricted to Bitcoin only.

3.4.2 Wasabi

While the name itself may conjure up images of delicious Japanese food, Wasabi is a desktop-based crypto wallet available on Windows, macOS, and Linux. So while it does not offer the convenience of having a mobile interface, it provides enhanced security features via the trustless CoinJoin process that makes individual Bitcoin transactions more secure by combining multiple coins from multiple people into a single transaction. By jumbling up the inputs and outputs, CoinJoins can obscure identifying information, making Wasabi a popular choice for the privacy-conscious. To further obfuscate transactions, the wallet routes them through the anonymizing Tor network, which helps conceal the users' IP addresses. Despite all these security features, please keep in mind that despite all these features, Wasabi is a hot wallet

3.4.3 Electrum

Electrum has been around since 2011, making it the aristocrat among the newer desktop wallets. It is available on Windows, Mac, Linux, and Android. It offers the advantage of occupying limited space on the computer's hard drive owing to the fact that it's a thin wallet client. This means it connects securely to other servers (instead of downloading the entire BTC blockchain) to verify Bitcoins balances and process payments.

Electrum uses a hierarchical deterministic wallet, which means a random 'seed' of 12 dictionary words is generated when you first launch the app. It derives the keys necessary to spend and receive BTC. Electrum displays the seed as you create your wallet and requires you to write it down. This means that if you lose access to this version of Electrum, you can easily reinstall it on another machine and use the seed to restore your BTC. Additionally, it offers encryption facilities. However, owing to its reliance on other servers, Electrum is extra vulnerable to hacking.

3.4.4 Mycelium

While Mycelium has both a desktop and mobile version, please remember that this is a Bitcoin-only wallet. It uses open-source software and relies on Simplified Payment Verification (SPV) technique, which allows it to confirm transactions without downloading the entire blockchain. However, if the online reviews are anything to go by, the mobile version has hefty transaction fees, so this is worth bearing in mind

3.4.5 Ownbit

This is a mobile-compatible digital non-custodial wallet that integrates both cold/offline and online functionalities. Ownbit is available on both iOS and Android devices. The dual online and offline/cold functionality ensures that the private keys are never connected to the internet. The private key is dynamically generated by the seed when needed, and it is not stored anywhere. The security model uses AES encryption and decryption, and the decryption speed is fast. The security enhancement-mode uses Scrypt-based hash cypher encryption and decryption, which is more effective against brute force. The source code is not freely available, so one has to install and try the code to check out its functionality.

Now middle of the path solution can be to use a combination of cold, crypto exchange-based/custodial, and hot wallets to distribute your crypto assets as you deem fit. Essentially, follow the old adage of- 'Don't put all your eggs in one basket. Indeed you could always invest in a second smartphone that functions only as a mobile crypto-cold wallet. When using a cell phone as a cold wallet, you would only turn it on when you want to make a transaction. The secondary phone acting as a cold wallet is then connected to your primary phone via Bluetooth or WiFi, and funds are transferred to your hot wallet for the transaction. After the transaction is made, the WiFi or Bluetooth connectivity is turned off, and the secondary phone is powered down. Ultimately whatever route you take, please remember not to put all your eggs in one basket (sorry for being repetitive) and pay attention to the nature of customer service the exchange or wallet offers.

CHAPTER 4

STRATEGY 1- HOLD ON FOR DEAR LIFE (HODL)

The simplest strategy for profiting from any asset class from equity to cryptos is to have no strategy at all (in a manner of speaking). Just Hold On for Dear Life (HODL). Or JHODL if you like. Now you must wonder why I am devoting an entire chapter to something that is really not a strategy in gawping at charts and other bells and whistles. But sometimes, the simplest things are the most difficult, and that is why I feel new investors need to have a deep understanding of what HODL is and how it can be the best thing you do as a beginner. I believe that by understanding the philosophy behind buying and holding, new Bitcoin investors will be able to weather market volatility better. Plus, I will share some handy tips to help you as you hang in.

4.1 Why Holding on For Dear Life (HODL) Is So Powerful

To be very fair, buying and holding are among the best things one can do when investing, including in cryptocurrency. And here, the operative word is 'investing' and not trading. For all their volatility, investing in cryptocurrencies should be treated like any other investment by following the motto-' Time in the market matters more than timing the market.' With this, one can hope to make gains without being stuck to charts 24/7. Since crypto markets are open 24/7, obsessing over every price move and all of Elon Musk's tweets could become very tiresome. That is not the path to sustainable investing. So for the sake of your sanity and sustainable investing, the first step is to **invest only the amount you can afford to lose without hurting yourself financially,** and the loss is something you can deal with at an emotional level. **Emotional preparedness is absolutely vital for investing**, especially when buying (and holding) Bitcoins.

In its relatively brief history, Bitcoin has had several pullbacks, including corrections of 50%-80%. All I can say is that those who held on tight during such stormy conditions certainly have reasons to rejoice. Of course, it is difficult to hang in when your investment loses 80% of its value. This is why the first and most important rule of Bitcoin investing is that be in $10 or $100,000 that you are putting in, make sure you are emotionally prepared never to see that money back again. Of course, tackling all the emotions that come with seeing your account go in the red (I have been there, and the first time around, it felt worse than the worst of my period cramps) is not made easy by a cacophony of 'market experts' who rush into declaring that Bitcoin is a scam or write its obituary. But please remember that the losses you see are only paper losses. Only when you panic and sell your Bitcoins, you get realised losses; you make actual losses. Peter McCormack, founder of the popular podcast, 'What Bitcoin Did,' (who incidentally got into BTC to buy weed off Silk Road and proceeded to make $1 million+ from his BTC holdings in 2017), recommends a buy-and-hold strategy as opposed to trading. It is worth bearing in mind that Bitcoin halvings have dominated the crypto market cycles. The ensuing Bitcoin availability crunch that happens every four years creates intense Fear Of Missing Out (FOMO) driven bull cycles, which have seen prices rise by thousands of per cent. These have been followed by severe pullbacks and subsequent 'crypto winters'- long periods of low Bitcoin prices. Many experts wrote off Bitcoin during 2017's crypto winter. So my motto is when in the business of Bitcoins- keep calm. And buy the dip.

4.2 Take A Sip and Buy The Dip

As a teetotaller, I can only sip on coffee or tea, and what you sip is up to you, but it's a good idea to buy the dip in the bitcoin space. Just imagine all those who bought Bitcoins during its sharpest pullbacks. While the famous American investor Warren Buffet is not into Bitcoins, I am a first believer in his philosophy, ' Be fearful when others are greedy and be greedy when others are fearful' as far as Bitcoins are concerned. Every sharp decline, including the steep declines we saw in May 2021, is a buying opportunity for me, and as of Oct 7, 20201, bitcoin is back at $50,000+. So I don't regret ignoring the doomsday predictions and buying the dip. And neither do most people who weathered Bitcoin's crypto winter of 2017 and accumulated Bitcoins even though experts were busy writing their usual BTC obituaries. To be honest, I also got a lot of other altcoins at a discount (but that is the topic for another book).

4.3 Dollar Cost Averaging (DCA)

Buying the dip is one common way of timing the market. Now, as I mentioned in section 4.1, time in the market usually outweighs timing the market. This is where dollar-cost averaging (DCA) comes into play. DCA entails putting in money in the market or an asset over time at set intervals. The input investment can be a fixed amount or depend on how much you can spare (or both). Set intervals can be weekly, bi-weekly or monthly. The best part is that you don't have to force yourself to top up your Bitcoin purchases. The following apps let you do this in an automated way:

4.3.1 Coinbase:

Coinbase is my go-to app for setting up crypto auto-saves. You can set up weekly or monthly recurring crypto purchases through Coinbase, and the set amount will be taken from your connected bank account. Please bear in mind that the transaction costs could be high in some countries.

4.3.2 Revolut:

As I mentioned, this is a money management app from the UK, but you can use your balances to buy cryptos for as little as £1. This app has a Vaults feature to round up your change and save these in the Vaults. You can use the same change rounding functionality to build up your Bitcoin balances. All you have to do is create a Vault, change its currency option to Bitcoin, and set your savings goal, e.g., I set mine to 1 BTC. Then make sure your 'Spare Change' option is turned on so every time you use your Revolut app to make a purchase either online or offline, the spare change is rounded off and used to buy Bitcoin fractions. While this may not be as intuitive as Coinbase's autosave functionality, I certainly like to have my crypto balances grow every time I make a purchase. Just bear in mind that you can turn on the spare changing option for just one vault.

4.3.3 Amber:

While the Amber app (https://amber.app/) is currently unavailable in the US, as of Oct 2021, its roll-out in the US is imminent. In the meantime, in the UK and other jurisdictions, users can start investing in Bitcoins from as little as $5 and do DCA by setting up recurring deposits. This is a Bitcoin-only app, so it could be beneficial to all those who are starting out.

4.3.4 Swan Bitcoin:

This is a Bitcoin-only app available only in the USA (as of October 2021). After verifying your identity and linking your US bank account, you can set up a fixed investment account and choose daily, weekly, monthly, or paycheck savings options as you deem fit. And that is not all. The Swan bitcoin app will buy more when the price goes down. An auto-withdrawals feature allows you to schedule periodic Bitcoin withdrawals to move a certain amount of Bitcoin to your private wallet. You can start with as little as $10 and save on transaction fees by pre-paying all your fees for the year right at the onset. Frankly, as a Brit, I am somewhat envious of this US-only Bitcoin DCA app.

4.3.5 Crypto.com:

This app allows for automated top-ups of a fixed amount at regular intervals (monthly, weekly or bi-weekly) for a fixed amount on a given day. The auto-transaction setup is intuitive, but the minimum auto-save amount is £40. One can start by investing a minimum of £40 in BTC either weekly, bi-weekly or monthly. At 2.99%, the transaction costs may be steep for some, but it would be worth checking out the transaction costs in your jurisdiction.

Some of the most prominent Bitcoin holders (also known as whales) are known to HODL-forever; they only accumulate and rarely sell their Bitcoins. This strategy may work for some people, but there may be times when you want to lay your hands on some extra cash or may even need some cash (I did a few months ago, and the window man was not going to take crypto payments). In that case, it may be advisable to cash out some of your Bitcoin holdings (say about 10%) when Bitcoin prices touch an All-Time High (ATH) or reach a certain predetermined point (I am waiting to cash out some of my eToro Bitcoin holdings at $90,000). With this extra cash, you can always buy the dip.

4.4 A Bit of Bot In Your Life?

To be very fair, bots are more common in the world of trading than investing. So you can skip this portion if you like. The apps listed in 4.3 are more than enough to support DCA investing. However, if you are looking for a slightly more high-tech solution and indeed want to explore trading at some point, then crypto bots could come in handy. Some bot-based options include:

4.4.1 HODL Bot:

A couple of centuries ago, William Shakespeare queried 'What's in a name?'. In the case of the HODLBot (https://www.hodlbot.io/), everything seems to be in the name. The website claims to support automated cryptocurrency investing. Additionally, users can index the market, create custom portfolios, and automatically rebalance their cryptocurrency portfolios. This one has a monthly subscription fee of $3 for accounts below $500 and $14/month for portfolios greater than $1000. Its most remarkable feature seems to be that it connects to several common crypto exchanges, and users can access advanced metrics to construct their crypto portfolios.

4.4.2 DCA Bot:

This is available through the Coinmate crypto trading platform (https://dcabot.online/), and it aims to support dollar-cost averaging (in this case, too, everything is in the name). Users can choose either buying with preset frequency (default) or stop-loss order strategy that processes the order when the exchange rate drops. The latter allows you to buy the dip, and you can grow your Bitcoin holdings steadily.

4.4.3 Heleum/Uphold:

Firstly, Uphold is not a crypto-trading bot as per se.In addition to buying and selling cryptocurrencies (and other asset classes such as metal), the app lets you set up automated cryptocurrency purchases/trades through the Heleum auto-trading app that runs on the Uphold platform via its open API. Access to this auto-trader needs you to have an Uphold account to begin with. Heleum continuously monitors exchange rates across the nine most traded national currencies and three top cryptocurrencies (Bitcoin, Litecoin, and Ethereum), instantly moving funds when rates are the most advantageous. So this app goes beyond the usual forex trading model of trading traditional fiat currency pairs (such as GBPUSD) and allows for trading between fiat-crypto pairs such as BTC-USD to accrue gains.

While bots are not strictly needed when one follows a HODL-only strategy. However, bots can come in handy when we want to undertake crypto diversification (more on that later).

CHAPTER 5

STRATEGY 2- EARN PASSIVE INCOME FROM YOUR BITCOINS

Several years ago, UK's banks had interest rates in the neighbourhood of 5%, which declined from 5.75% in July 2007 to 0.5 per cent by March 2009, with a further fall to 0.25 per cent in August 2016 owing to the 2008 subprime mortgage crisis. This financial crisis was the beginning of the end of high-interest rates in many countries. While 'investing' money in bank fixed deposits to earn interest was a common strategy in many parts of the world, this form of savings is becoming outmoded. Cryptocurrencies can offer the benefit of obtaining common interest via something known as 'staking.' Staking cryptocurrencies is a process that involves earning rewards and sometimes voting rights by committing one's crypto assets to support a blockchain network and confirm transactions. It's available with cryptocurrencies that use the proof-of-stake (POS) model to process payments. This is a more energy-efficient alternative to the proof-of-work model, which requires mining devices that use computing power to solve mathematical equations. So you must be wondering about its relevance here. You can use your Bitcoins to generate passive income via lending schemes and by providing liquidity through liquidity pools or even by locking in your Bitcoins for a given period to generate rewards.

5.1 Of Wrapping and Virtual Machines

While Etherum dominates the decentralised finance (DeFi) space, wrapping services such as Wrapped Bitcoin (WBTC) or the Ren Virtual Machine (renVM) can provide a passive income to Bitcoin holders. The former allows BTC to be deposited into a smart contract and used within the Ethereum-dominated DeFi ecosystem by minting ERC-20 compliant tokens, which are pegged to the value of Bitcoin. The Ren Virtual Machine (renVM) does the same via renBTC. With both renBTC and wrapped BTC, BTC holders can access the normal DeFi operations, including staking the way they would with ERC-20 and other POS tokens. In addition to staking, the modified BTC tokens can provide liquidity via decentralised exchanges (DEX) such as Uniswap.

5.2 Binance

You can use your Binance app as a Bitcoins saving account where you can lock up funds for a set period of time. Higher lock-up periods result in higher rewards. When you subscribe, Binance Savings will deduct the funds for the subscription from your exchange wallet and give you Flexible Savings assets. Additionally, Binance is now offering users up to 15% in annualized interest to users for lending their crypto assets.

5.3 Crypto.com

Crypto.com also allows users to earn Bitcoin rewards by locking up their BTC for a given period (usually 1-3 months). With BTC, you could earn up to 6.5% APY on a 3-month lock-up period, or 2% on a flexible basis if staking for under a month. However, all of these rates can change, so with Binance and Crypto.com, I would recommend checking the website or the app for the latest details.

5.4 Celsius

Founded in 2017, Celsius (https://celsius.network/) is one of the world's largest crypto earnings apps that facilitates the lending and borrowing of crypto assets, including Bitcoin. As of June 2021, it closed down its Uk service, which means it's no longer available for new Uk users. It is still available for users in the US and India (as of October 2021).

Celsius certainly has a laudable motto of "Unbank yourself." It allows users to earn up to 17% yield on their crypto holdings, including BTC. Users can also borrow cash at 1% using their crypto holdings as collateral. In addition to taking loans and earning yield (in terms of coins), earning passive income via savings account users can transfer crypto without fees. The app rewards the HODL strategy. Despite its regulatory difficulties, Celsius managed to raise $400 million in equity funding in Oct 2021. From its inception in 2017, the company has reached a valuation of $3 billion. However, regulators have suggested the firm carries out 'discretionary trading', including speculative trading with customer deposits. This indeed reminds me a bit of the shenanigan the big investment banks got up to in the lead up to the 2008 crisis. However, its goals and aims are indeed laudable, and the founder has a healthy startup track record. If successful, Celsius could have a good chance of being a viable substitute for traditional banks for retail investors.

5.5 BlockFi

BlockFi (https://blockfi.com/) is Celsius's closest competitor both in the crypto lending space and swimming in choppy regulatory waters. However, unlike Celsius, BlockFi is still available in the UK (as of Oct 2021) and in most jurisdictions except those facing international sanctions. It claims to have more than a million clients and $10 billion of institutional funds under its management. Apart from buying and selling Bitcoins, the app lets users earn around 8% in terms of its yields through its BlockFi Interest Account (BIA). The interests accrue daily and are paid monthly. However, as of October 2021, BIA is facing regulatory scrutiny in New Jersey, Texas, and Kentucky. BlockFi also offers its own credit card, which lets users earn up to 3.5% back in Bitcoins as cashback (however, the rewards are capped at $100).

5.6 Luno

On the lines of Celsius and BlockFi, Luno (https://www.luno.com/en) too lets its users earn interest on their BTC holdings (in addition to buying and selling cryptos through their platform). The app claims to offer 4% interest on BTC holdings per annum without any fixed time commitments or admin fees. They also provide educational content through their website. The Luno app is available on both Apple iOS and Android in most countries. Additionally, they have a referral program which means that people can earn Bitcoins by referring the app to other people.

5.7 Voyager Digital

Regarded as the Robinhood of cryptos, Voyager (https://www.investvoyager.com/) is the only fully regulated crypto-only brokerage in the USA. The company itself is publicly listed (under the stock ticker of $VYGVF). It offers around 10% interest on token deposits, including Bitcoin deposits.

5.8 Invictus Bitcoin Alpha (IBA) Fund:

In addition to Bitcoin investing, this Invictus Capital brainchild launched in 2020

(https://invictuscapital.com/en/bitcoin-alpha) aims to deliver additional yield by utilizing options and lending strategies, offering both downside protection and management of Bitcoin price volatility. It claims to aim for a Medium/high risk by accounting for BTC volatility whilst providing for a high return potential. It pursues a drawdown target of 10% per month via the purchase of an out-of-the-money put option. The IBA Fund goals to trace the value of bitcoin inside a predefined vary over any particular calendar month. The price of these put choices is backed by the sale of name choices within the area of 30% above the spot worth at the beginning of the month. This successfully means buyers shall be uncovered to cost features as much as 30% per thirty days, whereas being shielded from any extreme market drawdowns that will happen.

It remains to be seen whether these apps can append the traditional banking systems or not. Bitcoin lending, like all kinds of financial lending schemes, comes with its share of risks. For instance, in most cases, unlike bank deposits which are subject to statutory deposit insurance, crypto deposits are not insured. So while crypto lendings promise high yields, you could lose your assets if the platform goes bankrupt. Most centralised exchanges draw income from the lender assets by lending these to other crypto exchanges, institutional investors, and hedge funds via over-the-counter (OTC) transactions. This creates a counterparty risk because your lending platform provider may become insolvent if the counterparty to these trades fails to return the cryptocurrencies. While the platform will reduce this risk as much as possible by over-collateralizing the assets it lends out, it is not always transparent to most crypto lending users what risks the platform provider actually takes in OTC transactions. I recommend relying on well-known crypto lending platforms if you want to lend your Bitcoins to earn interest. For me, a good rule of thumb has been the quality of customer service, and I steer clear of service providers with a poor track record (so no Mode app for me). Another way of fortifying your crypto investments is via *diversification* (which I will discuss in the next chapter).

CHAPTER 6

STRATEGY 3- FUNDS ARE YOUR FRIENDS

Diversification is the key to successful investing. This is true as much in the crypto world as it is in the world of stocks and equities. In the world of stocks and bonds, An Exchange Traded Fund (ETF) is a basket of securities, shares of which are sold on an exchange. An ETF could contain all the shares listed on a stock market, such as FTSE 100 or all the stocks related to a given sector (e.g., the 5G sector). ETFs are regarded as one of the greatest inventions of the financial sector. You can get exposure to an entire market (e.g., the emerging markets) or an entire sector without having to buy every stock individually. This saves you the trouble of having to research every stock individually. The Walton family, owners of Walmart and one of the USA's wealthiest families invested the bulk of their multi-billion fortune in ETFs. This is how powerful ETFs are. While in September 2021, the Swiss regulators gave the green light to the country's first crypto asset fund called the Crypto Market Index Fund (open to qualified investors only). We don't have many widespread retail investor-friendly formal Bitcoin index tracker funds or Bitcoin ETFs. However, there are several crypto funds out there that will help you move beyond the world of Bitcoins and diversify your crypto holding pretty much the way ETFs and index tracker funds do for stocks and shares.

6.1 Common Crypto Funds

Some common platforms that provide crypto-funds or are crypto-funds (and crypto-funds, in this case, being a fund containing a number of cryptocurrencies) include:

6.1.1 EToro

Etoro is a social trading platform that also provides multi-asset brokerage facilities (https://www.etoro.com/). While eToro is well-known for its copy trading service, which can help many new investors and traders copy more experienced traders, it is rapidly expanding into the crypto space. It provides access to a variety of different cryptocurrencies via its CopyPortfolios. eToro Portfolios (CopyPortfolios) are investment vehicles that bundle together a collection of financial assets. It has several cryptocurrency-based CopyPortfolios including: CryptoPortfolio, CryptoEqual, CryptoTakeover. The former two grew by more than 400% from 2020-2021, while CryptoTakeover grew by 150%. However, these are highly volatile portfolios, and you have to invest $1000 upfront. If you want to cash your profits, you have to close the whole fund. However, they do provide exposure to a variety of cryptocurrencies besides the king of them all, Bitcoin. If you don't have $1000 to invest, you could always follow other investors and look for those with cryptocurrency-centric portfolios and essentially copy their trades for about $200-$500.

Here is my Medium post explaining why eToro is such an excellent platform for trading and investment, including crypto investments(https://bit.ly/3DsFSO8).

6.1.2 Ember Fund:

This is a crypto-only platform with a small selection of expert-curated crypto funds, including the Big Three fund, which contains BTC, ETH, and LTC. It prides itself as the first mobile app that allows users to buy into a managed cryptocurrency portfolio easily. The fund has a non-custodial nature, i.e., it does not hold user funds. The fund claims to bring institutional portfolio management expertise to retail crypto investors. Essentially it seeks to act as a crypto-only mobile hedge fund for retail investors. Marius Kraemer, a top-notch Bitcoin writer, acts as an advisor to the fund, and they also claim to use machine learning to put together their portfolios. The minimum balance requirement varies from $500 to $1000. Unlike eToro, this does not accept direct cash deposits. Instead, you have to transfer an equivalent amount of BTCs, which can be done by connecting one's Coinbase account. You need to put in a minimum of $500 to top up your fund. Unlike eToro, you don't have to close the entire fund to cash out your profits; you can liquidate your holdings in percentages (say 25%) to encash your profits. However, its inability to accept direct fiat transfers (unlike eToro) is rather tiresome, and it has been speculated that the Ember fund may offer fiat transfers in the future. The iOS app is quite intuitive to use.

6.1.3 Crypto 20 Index Fund (Invictus Capital)

Invictus Capital launched this cryptocurrency-based index fund launched in 2017, which tracks the top 20 cryptocurrencies by market cap (https://crypto20.com/en/). This fund offers the advantage of no broker fees, no exit fees, and no minimum investment. This is a tokenized fund where seed funding is used for buying the underlying assets. The fund caps each coin at around 10% of the portfolio, providing diversification.

Its greatest ETF-Esque feature is its management fees of 0.5% (comparable to the fees levied by traditional ETFs). While the fund saw more than an 800% increase from 2020-2021, from 2017 to the present, the fund, on average, grew by 37%. This period accounts for the crypto market crash of 2017, when Bitcoin had a very sharp retracement. Additionally, one can add money at regular intervals, thus achieving dollar-cost averaging.

6.1.4 Bitwise 10 Crypto Index Fund

This fund was launched in 2017 and is currently administered by Theorem Fund Services

(https://www.bitwiseinvestments.com/funds/Bitwise-10). This seeks to allow investors to gain exposure to Bitcoin and other leading cryptocurrencies by tracking the ten most highly valued cryptocurrencies weighted by market capitalization. The fund is rebalanced monthly, and its shares are tradable in brokerage accounts using ticker "BITW" and maybe of interest from those with a traditional stock market investment background. The fund has grown more than 400% since its inception. The Bitcoin ETF space is expanding, and beyond 2021, it will be worth keeping an eye on the developments in this area. As of October 2021, J.P. Morgan and Wells Fargo have launched Bitcoin funds, although they are only available to their wealthy clients in the former case.

6.1.5 Grayscale Bitcoin Trust (GBTC)

GBTC can be best described as a closed-end grantor trust rather than an ETF or a mutual fund. Owing to its structure, it issues a fixed number of shares when it goes public, and then those shares are traded "over-the-counter" (OTC). While GBTC shares are intended to follow the price of

Bitcoin (based on the CoinDesk Bitcoin Price Index), it must be borne in mind that now new shares are created when assets flow into the fund. Further, GBTC has a management fee of 2%, which is way too high for my liking. As of late October 2021, each share of the Grayscale Bitcoin Trust represents 0.00093535 bitcoins. However, this number is not fixed as closed-end trusts such as GBTC can trade at a discount or premium to their underlying assets (unlike ETFs). Unlike ETFs, GBTC tracks the supply and demand of Bitcoins as opposed to tracking the underlying asset value. In 2021, the value of the units fell to a 25 % discount to the underlying bitcoins, which is quite a dismal performance. However, it is being speculated that GBTC wants to move from being a trust to an ETF. Such a conversion could eliminate the premium/discount issue which has dogged GBTC for so long. While Bitcoin futures ETF are now in existence (see 6.1.7) for more details, it will be interesting to see if GBTC decides to join the futures race or come back as a Bitcoin spot ETF.

6.1.6 Purpose Bitcoin ETF

Like conventional ETFs, Bitcoin ETFs seek to mimic Bitcoin price action. The Purpose Bitcoin ETF is the first physically settled Bitcoin ETF that does not need investors to hold their crypto assets in digital wallets. Unlike Bitcoin futures, this ETF buys actual Bitcoins, which the investors can trade seamlessly and get tax benefits based on their target jurisdiction. However, it must be borne in mind that the ETF is only available to Canadian investors and is yet to be approved by the Security Exchange Commission (SEC).

6.1.7 SEC-Approved Bitcoin Futures ETFs (launched in October 2021)

There is an adage that says, 'when it rains, it pours. This is undoubtedly true in the case of SEC-approved Bitcoin ETFs. It took the better part of a decade before Bitcoin ETFs were approved by the SEC, but when they were, two were launched in October 2021. The ProShares Bitcoin Strategy ETF (trading under the name $BITO) is a Bitcoin futures ETF that made its debut on the New York Stock Exchange (NYSE) on October 19, 2021. It jumped up by more than 4% on its debut. $BITO's annual management fee is 1% which is a bit too expensive for my liking. The fund tracks CME bitcoin futures, or contracts speculating on the future price of bitcoin, rather than the crypto itself (cash-settled, front-month Bitcoin futures – contracts with the shortest time to maturity.), which means the ETF price could be different from the actual asset (BTC). This fund seeks to capture gains via exposures to Bitcoin price changes via short-term bitcoin futures contracts, meaning that it has to sell expiring contracts and buy new ones regularly. In this sense, $BITO and other futures-based Bitcoin ETFs are analogous to the United States Oil Fund (USO), which also invests in futures and does not accurately track oil prices. While the debut is inspiring, nothing can be said about its future with any measure of certainty, with many investors suggesting they would rather buy actual Bitcoins (including billionaire Mark Cuban). Close on heels of $BITO came Valkyrie's Bitcoin Strategy ETF ($BTF), the second exchange-traded fund allowing U.S. investors direct exposure to Bitcoin futures. On October 22, 2021, it debuted on NYSE but could not match $BITO's stunning debut. Instead, $BTF fell by 3% on its launch, and after its initial rise, $BITO too had a tumble. For me, the Bitcoin ETF space is something to watch for as opposed to rushing in (so I am doing a Mark Cuban at present).

It must be borne in mind that Bitcoin-based ETFs and funds are still far and few, although many funds do seek to follow the performance of stocks that are disproportionately affected by Bitcoin prices (more on this in the next chapter, chapter 7). However, as of 2021, efforts are underway to launch more Bitcoin ETFs, including Bitcoin spot ETFs. As of October 2021, Cathie Woods of Ark Investments has teamed up with 21Shares US LLC (an affiliate of Zug, Switzerland-based 21Shares AG) to launch the ARK 21Shares Bitcoin Futures Strategy ET (ARKA). If approved by the SEC, ARKA will invest in Bitcoin futures. After withdrawing an offer to establish a Bitcoin ETF in 2019, Bitwise has restarted its attempt to launch a Bitcoin spot ETP in late 2021. On October 16, 2021, Jacobi Asset Management received authorization from the Guernsey Financial Services Commission (GFSC) to launch the world's first tier-1 Bitcoin ETF. The Jacobi Bitcoin ETF will be listed on Cboe Europe, one of the largest pan-European equity exchanges, subject to Financial Conduct Authority (FCA) listing approval. While ETFs make a lot of sense when one wants exposure to an entire industry, a given stock market (such as the S&P 500), or a sector such as the emerging markets, their utility in the Bitcoin space is debatable. However, such ETFs may work well with people who have a long-term view and want their exposure to bitcoins to sit side by side with their exposure to other asset classes such as gold ETFs. Through these, they can certainly get rid of the hassle of folding onto private keys and such. However, it should be borne in mind that ETFs are not typically available to British investors and we Brits usually rely upon platforms such as eToro to get ETF exposure. As of October 2021, these Bitcoin futures ETFs are yet to be made available on eToro.

For those of you wishing to construct your own cryptocurrency portfolios, Wisely (https://wisly.io/portfolio/) is one of the world's first cryptocurrency trackers that provides detailed cryptocurrency metrics to facilitate investment and trading decisions. In particular, bitcoins in general and ETFs that could offer direct exposure to bitcoins is a very rapidly evolving field. You can always follow me on my Medium page to get updated news and analysis on cryptocurrency-related topics: https://minerva-data-owl.medium.com/

6.2 Bots Are Back

I previously introduced crypto trading bots to you. But now is the time to expand on them. Crypto trading bots are computer programs that automate cryptocurrency trading. While beginner investors are best advised to stay away from active trading, some trading bots provided to FinTech companies could provide crypto diversification without being stuck trying to figure out what to buy and what to sell. Here are some bot-based crypto diversification options with considering

6.2.1 Crypto Autopilot (OSOM finance)

OSOM Finance is an Estonia-based fintech, and it provides automated crypto trading via its Crypto Autopilot fund. This fund works on a hedge fund principle and tries to maximize profits by picking and choosing the best performers. It's a no-frills option for inexperienced, first-time crypto users who want to diversify their crypto holdings in an automated manner. The charges are 10% off the profits. While it accepts both BTC and bank transfers, the latter can take a couple of days, so please bear that in mind. I found their support staff to be prompt and helpful, which is always a plus, in my opinion.

6.2.2 Coinrule

This is an option for more advanced users. Coinrule allows you to design your own bot and set your own trading rules based on coin type or percentage, or price. Unlike OSOM, it offers the convenience of connecting to crypto exchanges such as Binance to implement trading strategies. I would certainly pass this one unless you have experience in trading, cryptocurrencies, and algorithm design.

Outside of crypto funds, the ultimate tools of investment and diversification- stocks and ETFs can come in handy, allowing us to benefit from the Bitcoin gyrations.

CHAPTER 7

STRATEGY 4- STOCK MARKET CAN HELP YOU PROFIT FROM THE BITCOIN BOOM

For all its decentralization, Bitcoin is affected by external factors ranging from changes in national policies to tweets. Bitcoin, with its $1 trillion caps too, influences the broader market trends. In September 2021, when the global stock market had a downturn, crypto prices, including Bitcoin prices, saw a bear run. As of October 2021, both stock prices and Bitcoin prices are in a strong bull phase. As the institutional adoption and mainstreaming of bitcoins grows, so will the correlation of its price action with other asset classes and, notably, stocks. Additionally, macro-level developments such as those related to inflation could influence Bitcoin prices. This opens up a new avenue of volatility and, therefore, an opportunity from Bitcoin price movements, albeit indirectly by investing or trading in Bitcoin-centric shares and ETFs.

The stock value of publicly listed companies is influenced directly by Bitcoins as a result of large BTC holdings (e.g., Tesla) or involvements (such as Bitcoin mining) and indirectly as a consequence of being a part of the Bitcoin ecosystem's food chain (e.g., companies that provide chips and components for Bitcoin computational resources, energy companies). Blockchain technology is one of the most transformational technologies of the 21 st century, and Bitcoin mining is a computationally intense endeavour (see chapter 1 and chapter 2). While the nature of Bitcoin mining poses challenges and raises many concerns, it is transformational technologies like these that galvanise the world (and provide investors multiple pathways to profiting while they continue their steady march on). Three major ways in which investors can leverage the stock market to benefit from Bitcoin price movements include:

7.1 Companies With A Direct Bitcoin Connection

While these are not formal designations, in this category lie the companies that are either involved with Bitcoin mining and/or have large Bitcoin holdings.

7.1.1 Riot Blockchain ($RIOT)

Bitcoin bear runs usually result in this NASDAQ company being read the riot act (pun intended). But then that is the nature of the being, or rather Riot Blockchain ($RIOT). Riot Blockchain, Inc. is a Bitcoin mining company. It states that it seeks to support the Bitcoin blockchain by expanding large-scale mining in the US and by improving both the infrastructural capacity and hash rate. Their holdings include the Whinstone U.S. facility in Rockdale, Texas (a wholly-owned subsidiary of Riot Blockchain and consists of the single largest Bitcoin mining and hosting facility in North America) and hosted miners at Coinmint LLC's Massena, New York facility. According to the company, their production increased three times in 2021 (compared to 2020) and holds around 194 million in Bitcoin. It would be an understatement to say that $RIOT's price actions are substantial if not wholly influenced by Bitcoin price gyrations and Bitcoin-related news.

7.1.2 Marathon Digital Holdings ($MARA)

$MARA is another Bitcoin proxy. In 2021 it made news as a result of its large-scale Bitcoin purchases (the same for Tesla, which we will cover in section 7.2). However, unlike Tesla, $MARA is directly involved with the business of Bitcoins. Marathon Digital Holdings aims to build the most significant Bitcoin mining operation in North America at one of the lowest energy costs. Its Bitcoin focus seems to be paying off. As of late October 2021, the stock gained more than 2000% over the last 12 months, earning the average rating from Wall Street analysts of a Strong Buy. Analysts predict 2022 to be a year of further stock price increases. However, you must always do your research before investing in a stock.

7.1.3 Cannan ($CAN)

While Cannan is listed on NASDAQ under the ticker $CAN, it's a China-based computer hardware manufacturer that manufactures Bitcoin mining ASIC units. Canaan's fortunes have seen boom-bust cycles which coincide with changes in Bitcoin popularity. As of 2021, $CAN is riding high on the ongoing Bitcoin bull run. However, $CAN saw sharp retracements in its stock prices both in June and September 2021, as well as a nearly 76% revenue decline from 2020-2021. However, from 2021, $CAN has embarked on Bitcoin mining itself along with selling Bitcoin mining equipment to Kazakhstan. However, if China's Bitcoin ban and a crackdown on tech companies (including those listed on US exchanges) open, a can of worms for $CAN remains to be seen.

7.1.4 Hut8 Mining ($HUT)

Headquartered in Canada, $HUT is one of the largest cryptocurrency mining companies in North America. $HUT is located in Canada's energy-rich province of Alberta, which contributes to it having one of the highest installed capacity rates in the industry. Additionally, $HUT holds more self-mined Bitcoin than any crypto miner or publicly-traded company globally. In addition to Bitcoin mining, it also offers white-label high-performance computer hosting, as well as income generation via its Bitcoin reserves. Hut 8 was the first publicly traded miner on the

TSX and the first Canadian miner to be listed on The Nasdaq Global Select Market. While it $HUT has a sterling technical performance, it does run the risk of being caught up in a regulatory crossfire between Canada and the USA.

7.1.5 Argo Blockchain ($ARGO)

Argo Blockchain is a UK-based cryptocurrency mining company. Unlike most other Bitcoin mining companies, $ARGO champions the use of renewable energy to support mining operations and has energy-efficient mining facilities located in Texas, USA. In chapter 2, I mentioned how Bitcoin's carbon footprint was a cause of concern and even resulted in a massive pullback in Bitcoin prices in the middle of 2021. In 2021, Argo partnered with another eco-friendly mining firm DMG Blockchain to create Terra Pool — a Bitcoin mining pool consisting of a hash rate derived from both company's hydroelectric power sources. As the debate on Bitcoin's energy consumption heats up (no pun intended), its focus on renewable energy could give $ARGO an extra edge over other cryptocurrency firms.

7.1.6 Hive Blockchain ($HIVE)

Hive blockchain was the first publicly traded crypto miner to make it to the Toronto Venture Exchange in 2017. In addition to providing crypto equipment, validation blockchain transactions, $HIVE also seeks to act as a bridge between the traditional financial and crypto space. In October 2021, $HIVE ordered 6,500 Bitcoin mining machines from Cannan, which arguably provided a boost to both companies. The company further announced its foray into the non-fungible token (NFT) space, a move that can be very rewarding in the future.

7.1.7 Bitfarms ($BITF)

$BITF operates blockchain computing centres that provide computing power to cryptocurrency networks such as the Bitcoin blockchain. It earns a fee from each network for securing and processing transactions. Additionally, it is hydroelectricity powered, making its energy sourcing relatively cheaper and cleaner. As I discussed before, the use of clean energy for powering mining operations could act as a USP. It saw an increase in Bitcoin mining in late 2021, which combined with $BTC's 2021 all-time price highs is a positive scenario. However, its move to establish a bitcoin mega-mining farm in Argentina has raised concerns for legislators. Legislative concerns usually act as stock price downers; hence this is worth bearing in mind. However, the use of clean energy for Bitcoin mining is a trend worth keeping an eye on. In late 2020, the Bitcoin mining company Compass Inc announced the opening of its new mining centre in Ontario, which is going to rely mostly on green energy (in the form of hydroelectric and nuclear power).

Given their direct involvement with Bitcoins and the Bitcoin infrastructure, the prices of these stocks are strongly affected by Bitcoin price moves. So expect a great going during a Bitcoin bull run and be gut-punched during a Bitcoin bear run. Indeed the stock prices of these stocks closely mirrored the Bitcoin price action from July 2021- August 2021

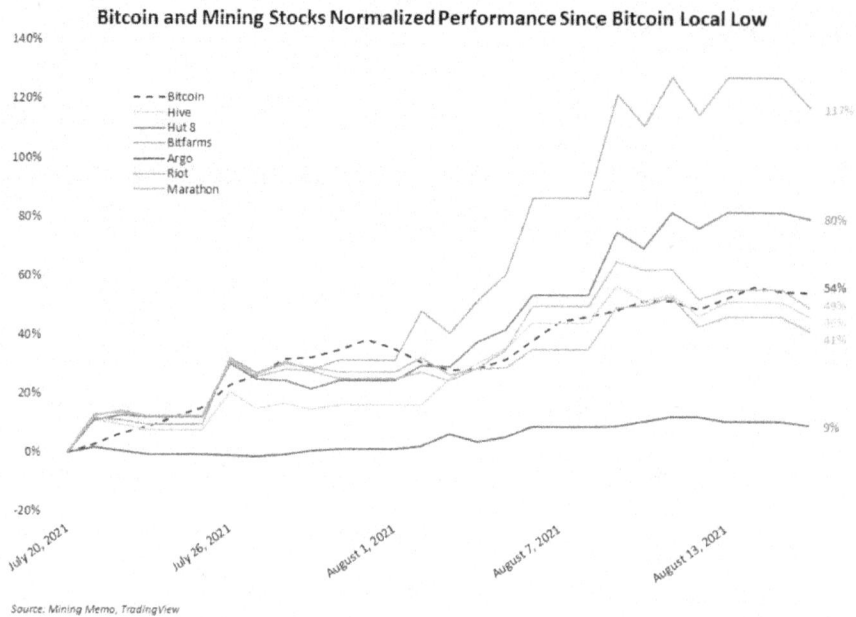

Bitcoin and Mining Stocks Normalized Performance Since Bitcoin Local Low

Source. Mining Memo, TradingView

Figure 6: Price Action of Bitcoins viz a viz Crypto Mining Stocks (taken from: https://compassmining.io/education/mining-stocks-bitcoin-recovery-comparison-q3-2021/)

Even though these companies followed the Bitcoin price action, considerable differences remain between individual stocks. For instance, in this period, while Bitfarms and Hut8 outperformed Bitcoin, $HIVE, $RIOT, and $MARA kept pace while Argo Blockchain fell behind. Clearly, not all blockchain company stocks are created equal. The boom-bust routine of these stocks may be a bit too overwhelming, especially if you are a beginner. However, with increased institutional acceptance, there is a battalion of companies benefitting from Bitcoins directly or indirectly. Focusing on them could provide exposure to both Bitcoins price changes and diversification.

7.2 Companies That Benefit From Blockchain Technology/Bitcoins

These companies have nothing to do with Bitcoins directly. But these are indirectly intertwined with Bitcoins, such as by supporting Bitcoin transactions. This is a fairly broad church of companies with direct Bitcoin involvement, even though the magnitude of the said involvement varies, which is likely to influence the link between stock and Bitcoin prices.

7.2.1 Tesla ($TSLA)

Elon Musk made quite a splash in early 2021 with his $1.5 billion purchase of Bitcoins and has been making a lot of news with his subsequent cryptocurrency-related tweets (which do impact the price action). However, 2021 has been Tesla's year of phenomenal growth. In October 2021 itself, $TSLA stock prices nearly doubled and crossed the $1200 threshold by early November on the news of $TSLA supplying electric vehicles to Hertz. $TSLA is now a trillion-dollar enterprise, and gaining exposure to this stock either through direct holdings or ETFs (such as Cathie WOod's ARK ETFs) does seem to be a good idea for both Bitcoin and non-Bitcoin aficionados.

7.2.2 Microstrategy ($MSTR)

$MSTR follows the strategy of some of its cash and future cash flow in alternative assets such as stocks, bonds, commodities, and Bitcoins. The Bitcoin investments are of note as in 2020. The company took over $2 billion in debt so that it could buy over 100,000 bitcoins for more than $2.7 billion. $MSTR's market cap has increased from $1.15 to $6.5

billion by 2021. As of 2021, $MSTR owns approximately 105,000 Bitcoins. Arguably Bitcoin prices will continue to influence the company's financial well-being, which in turn may influence stock prices. From 2020-2021, MSTR's stock price increased, mirrored Bitcoin price increases.

7.2.3 AMD and NVIDIA

Both the semiconductor companies $NVIDIA and $AMD don't deal with cryptocurrencies directly. But these chipmakers are the leading designers of graphics processing units (GPUs). Best known for powering high-end video game graphics, GPUs now enable computing-intensive applications such as data centres, artificial intelligence, and the creation of crypto assets. GPUs are an integral part of the cryptocurrency mining ecosystem. Both Nvidia and AMD recently announced acquisitions that will likely further cement their positions as leaders in chip technology. Nvidia is trying to purchase ARM Holdings, a licensor of chip architecture design for data centres and smartphones, and AMD is planning to acquire field-programmable chip leader Xilinx

7.2.5 Robinhood Markets ($HOOD)

2021 has been quite a year for Robinhood. It had a meteoric IPO followed by a sharp price tumble. While its zero-commission trading feature has made it a popular app among US retail traders, its entry into the cryptocurrency sphere could provide an additional boost. Robinhood shares rose by more than 10% on the news of the app enabling its crypto-wallet for the sale and purchase of cryptocurrencies such as Bitcoin. The sky is truly the limit as Robinhood can combine its commission-free model with scaling the number of cryptocurrencies on the platform, thereby gaining a massive competitive advantage over both traditional and decentralized exchanges. With this, it can become the go-to app for both stock and crypto traders.

7.2.6 Square ($SQ)

Square's tryst with Bitcoin goes back to 2017 when its Cash App started offering the Bitcoin trading feature. This early move certainly benefited $SQ in 2020 and 2021, and as crypto transactions increase, the stock may well benefit in the future. Additionally, $SQ has been on an acquisition spree in 2021, so this is one crypto-influenced stock worth looking at.

7.2.7 Coinbase ($COIN)

Coinbase had a splashy IPO in April 2021 with a sharp increase in its stock value post-IPO (and a sharp decline after that) and remains one of the most popular crypto exchanges around. However, the $COIN stock price is strongly influenced by Bitcoin price moves. Analysts have calculated that more than 80% correlation exists between $COIN stock prices and Bitcoin prices. So investors may need to be prepared for boom-bust price moves akin to the stocks of 7.1. However, as of October 2021, a disconnect emerged between Bitcoin's ATH prices and a decline in $COIN stock. However, this failure is being attributed to hiccups such as Coinbases's run-in with the SEC and a hacking scandal. Given the increasing popularity of cryptos and rising Coinbase users, this is a stock worth keeping an eye on.

7.2.8 Paypal ($PYPL)

In the footsteps of $SQ, PYPL too has enabled crypto purchases within its wallet (Venmo) from 2021. With the most users of any peer-to-peer money movement app, Venmo could become a leading cryptocurrency platform with this new feature. It serves as a solid access point for investors who wish to buy major cryptocurrencies and then uses them to purchase altcoins or access decentralized finance applications.

This is quite a cast crew of companies involved in the Bitcoin space, either directly or indirectly. The role of Bitcoin prices in influencing the stock price movement of these is going to vary by the magnitude of their Bitcoin exposure and dependency. Now, if you are anything like me and don't like to pick individual stocks, then exchange-traded funds (ETFs) are your friends. Specifically, you can invest in ETFs that focus on blockchain technology or benefit from it.

7.3 Blockchain Exchange Traded Funds (ETFs)

While one does not need to have an advanced maths degree or a Mensa-IQ to pick the right stocks and shares, far too many of us lack the time needed to research stocks. This is where exchange-traded funds (ETS) come in. In this section, I am going to weigh in on ETFs as most people understand them- a type of security that tracks an index, sector, commodity, or other asset and how these can help you benefit from Bitcoin price actions.

7.3.1 Bitcoin World Wide Smart Portfolio by eToro:

I have waxed lyrical about eToro previously in the book, and it is one of the platforms through which British investors can gain access to ETFs. The Bitcoin World Wide Smart Portfolio is a Market Copy Portfolio provided by eToro rather than an actual ETF. 75% of this portfolio comprises stocks that are influenced by Bitcoin price movements (many of the companies mentioned in 7.1 and 7.2) are a part of this Copy Portfolio. The remaining 25% is BTC. As with other Market Copy Portfolios, you have to invest $1000 upfront. If you want to cash your profits, you have to close the whole fund. In late 2021, its 2-year return stood at around 7%, but it has a lower risk factor (of 6) as compared to the other cryptocurrency-only Copy Portfolios.

7.3.2 Amplify Transformational Data Sharing ETF (BLOK)

BLOK is one of the oldest blockchain-centric ETFs out there, with $1 billion under management. This is an actively managed fund that seeks to provide total return by investing at least 80% of its net assets in the equity securities of companies that are involved with blockchain technology. Some of its holdings include Paypal, Square, Coinbase, and

Microstrategy. As of late 2021, its 52-week price range varied from $24.53 to $62.94.

7.3.3 Siren Nasdaq NexGen Economy ETF (BLCN)

BLCN, established in 2018, is a passively managed ETF with nearly $278.4 million in management (expense ratio 0.68%) that seeks to match the performance of the Nasdaq Blockchain Economy Index. The Nasdaq Blockchain Economy Index comprises stocks of companies with a market cap greater than $200 million that support blockchain technology or utilize it for their businesses. BLCN has a proprietary screening methodology based on which companies are assigned a 'blockchain score,' which quantifies the ability of a company to benefit from the blockchain technology. BLCN is a well-diversified ETF comprising companies including Coinbase and Square. The top 10 holdings account for just 20% of its overall assets. In addition to sector diversification, the fund is geographically diversified as well. The U.S. accounts for 53% of assets, with the rest coming from other nations, including Japan (13%) and China (13%).

7.3.4 First Trust Indxx Innovative Transaction & Process ETF (LEGR)

Also launched in 2018, LEGR is another cryptocurrency-focused ETF that tracks the performance of the Indxx Blockchain Index. This index focuses on all available blockchain companies and ensures that each holding meets specific size, liquidity, and trading minimums. It then applies a score of 1 for companies actively developing blockchain technology, 2 for companies actively using blockchain technology, and 3 for companies actively exploring blockchain technology. The index then only includes mostly larger market capitalization companies scoring 1 or 2, giving 50% of the weighting to firms scoring 1 and 50% to those scoring 2. Companies scoring three are excluded altogether. The portfolio is capped at 100 stocks, and the index is rebalanced and reconstituted twice a year. Through its stock selection strategy, the fund has exposure to a variety of sectors (including technology and financial services) and geographies (USA, India, China, to name a few).

7.3.5 Simplify US Equity PLUS GBTC ETF (SPBC)

Unlike the previously mentioned funds, which focus on blockchain stocks, SPBC aims to follow the 110% Bitcoin exposure strategy. This it does by having a 100% equity focus (like the other funds) topped up with an additional 10% bitcoin exposure. Most of SPBC's equity exposure is via its iShares Core S&P 500 ETF (IVV holding), which is one of the major S&P 500 ETFs. Additionally, SPBC also invests a little of its assets into E-mini S&P 500 Futures, which provides much more exposure to the broader market than the ETF can provide. That allows it to invest an additional 10% to a maximum of 15% in the Grayscale Bitcoin Trust

7.3.6 The Global X Blockchain ETF (BKCH)

Compared to other ETFs mentioned here, BKCH only had about $54 million under management and a relatively lower expense ratio of 0.5%. BKCH tracks the performance of the Solactive Blockchain Index, a collection of stocks that have operations that utilize or benefit from digital assets and blockchain technologies. It divides the companies into three groups: 1.) "pure-play" stocks that derive at least 50% of revenues from blockchain activities; 2.) "pre-revenue" firms whose primary business is in blockchain technology but don't yet generate revenue; and 3.)

"diversified" companies that generate less than 50% of revenues from blockchain activities. The index is weighted by free-float market cap, but it also has a few rules it enforces at each rebalancing. No component can account for more than 12% of the portfolio and no less than 0.3%. All stocks with a weighting of greater than 4.5% can't collectively account for more than 45% of the portfolio, with the remainder capped at 4.5%. And pre-revenue firms and diversified companies can't make up more than 10% of the firm collectively, and individually can't be weighed any more than 2%. Consequently, in terms of its equity selection, BKCH is technology-centric.

7.3.7 VanEck Digital Transformation ETF (DAPP)

This is another global-scale passive ETH that tracks the performance of the MVIS Global Digital Assets Equity Index, which invests in companies participating in the digital assets economy. Holdings are believed to have the potential to generate at least half of their annual revenue from digital assets. This is a relatively smaller portfolio with a technological focus and global coverage. This ETF was launched in April 2021, so it is still at its initial stages.

In addition to the blockchain focussed ETFs, you can also take a look at Cathie Wood's ARK ETFs. While these actively managed funds are not blockchain-centric as the ETFs mentioned in section 7.1.3, they do have good exposure to many of the companies mentioned in 7.1.2.

CHAPTER 8

FINAL THOUGHTS

While you may have missed buying $BTC at $1000 but with the increased mainstreaming of Bitcoins, the post-2021 era is likely to provide a wide variety of opportunities both in terms of Bitcoin investments and investments in related areas. Bitcoin touched an all-time-highs in 2021, and many financial experts now predict Bitcoin is on its way to breaching the $100,000. In fact, the famous fund manager, Cathie Woods, the Founder and CEO of ARK Investments, suggests Bitcoin could also go up to $500,000. Here is the price-only forecasting model that I developed using historical price data: Is Bitcoin Headed to $100,000? This, too, indicates the prices going up to $100K by the summer of 2022. However, like all other forecasts, these forecasts need to be taken with a pinch of salt. But even with all the institutional interest, Bitcoin is likely to remain a volatile asset with the potential to provide an interesting avenue for diversification.

One of the other things in Bitcoin's favour is that it is widely being touted as a hedge against inflation. In fact, in early October 2021, JP Morgan (one of earlier Bitcoin detractors) stated that Bitcoin could be a better hedge against inflation than gold. Certainly, as inflationary fears pile on, institutional investors are pouring into Bitcoins. In the first quarter of 2021, Coinbase recorded more than 200 billion in crypto purchases from 8000 institutional investors. The rising inflationary fears stem from improving economic conditions, and enormous stimulus packages have increased the global money supply. Unlike fiat currencies such as the Pound Sterling or the US dollar, Bitcoins can't be devalued by a government or a central bank distributing too much of them. If you remember from chapter 1, there are only 21 million Bitcoins in all that exists. Once they are gone, they are gone. Each bitcoin is divisible into 100m satoshis, helping growth through smaller units of account as the value appreciates. Now Bitcoins replacing gold as a store of value may seem odd to some people. After gold is a physical entity that most of us have seen or even worn around our necks. However, it is this physical nature that poses a challenge when gold is a store of value- its physicality that makes it hard to transport and is vulnerable to government control. In contrast, you could walk around with Bitcoins on your phone. We just have a decade of data on Bitcoins so how things play out, in the long run, remains to be seen. Of course, from 2020-21, gold prices declined, whereas by now, you all know about Bitcoin's meteoric rise. But if the inflationary pressures increase and recession sets in, then I expect more and more people to flee to Bitcoins. Ultimately I am bullish on Bitcoin investing. In addition to all the information I have provided in this book, I would also like the newly minted Bitcoin aficionados to take some basic precautions

8.1 Common Sense Ways of Protecting Yourself When Investing In Bitcoins (or Any Other Asset)

These common-sense financial self-defence tips apply across the board- be it Bitcoins or stocks. The first golden rule is that **NEVER invest any more than what you can afford to lose**. Nope. Never. I don't care how many media stories are put out there telling us about how someone invested their entire life savings in a cryptocurrency and became a millionaire. For me, the risk is just too much. For every one person who becomes wealthy this way, so many others end up in poverty. So I don't recommend such a gamble. Second, **do not ever borrow money to buy Bitcoins** or any other investment. Investing in Bitcoins (and other assets) needs to come from your budget and not from borrowings. Luckily as described in this book, there are plenty of tools to build up your Bitcoin investments without breaking the bank.

Another risk factor associated with Bitcoin investments is the sheer volume of scams floating about. This is compounded by the fact that so many scammers are geniuses when it comes to using social media for furthering their nefarious agendas. A detailed overview of all the crypto scams out there would need a completely new book. However, it is worth keeping in mind that if something sounds too good to be true, it probably is. So all those people on social media and those who inbox you with offers of doubling your cryptos may well be scammers. I recommend giving them a miss. Always do some research on the background of companies and individuals in the crypto space before you part with either your fiat or crypto resources. Most well-known institutions and individuals will have a social media presence. There are times you may be contacted by people and/or SM pages claiming to be linked to Wall Street Bets. The real Wall Street Bets exist only on Reddit. Another thing worth avoiding are the Telegram groups that provide trading and/or pump-and-dump schemes. It is always better to do your research than rely on signalling services. At any rate, for beginners, Bitcoin investments with a medium to long-term perspective is preferable to trading. Of course, the most important thing to keep in mind on your investing journey is to remember the virtue of patience and prudence.

I will be grateful for your feedback, and please drop me a line at minerva.data.lab@gmail.com. Further, the Bitcoin and cryptocurrency space are rapidly evolving. You can always follow me on my Medium page to get updated news and analysis on cryptocurrency-related topics: https://minerva-data-owl.medium.com/

You can download your whistle-stop no-fluff guide to profiting from Bitcoins in 2021 and beyond: https://minerva-ea911.gr8.com/. This will be your primer on what to do and what not to do in order to succeed on your Bitcoin journey.